SPIRIT AND POWER

God's Presence and Answers to Prayer in Pavel Goia's Journey

PAVEL GOIA
WITH
KELLY MOWRER

Safeliz

Title: **In the Spirit and Power**
Subtitle: God's Presence and Answers to Prayer in Pavel Goia's Journey
Authors: Pavel Goia with Kelly Mowrer

Project Design - Editorial Safeliz
CEO: Mario Paulo Martinelli
CFO: Sergio Mato Rhiner
Editing: Mennen Pearl Talibong and José David Pallas
Cover Design and Layout: Bezalel&Aoliabe
Cover photo background: Getty Images

Editorial Safeliz, S. L. · Pradillo, 6 · Pol. Ind. La Mina
E-28770 · Colmenar Viejo, Madrid, Spain · Tel.: [+34] 91 845 98 77
admin@safeliz.com · www.safelizbibles.com

ISBN: 978-84-7208-900-6

June 2022: 1st edition
IMP16

ENDORSEMENTS

"I like to read books that go beyond my thoughts and touch my heart. IN THE SPIRIT AND POWER is one of them. It's inspiring to see how Pavel Goia learned to live by faith, depend on prayer, and believe in modern miracles. It's amazing to see how it impacted his life, family, and ministry and especially opened doors for revival and mission. Pavel Goia is someone who learned to count the blessings, and now he's also sharing these blessings. Read this book full of confidence that God never changes, and Pavel's story can be your story through the power of prayer."

Erton C. Köhler, *Executive Secretary, General Conference of Seventh-day Adventists*

"Pavel Goia has lived a life of faith and prayer and writes out of a crucible of the deep experiences of God. His remarkable stories of God's miracles will inspire you with a deeper walk with the Lord. Pavel beautifully weaves prayer principles with amazing stories in a tapestry of life-changing faith. I highly recommend IN THE SPIRIT AND POWER as an aid to your spiritual journey."

Mark A. Finley, *Assistant to the President for Evangelism, General Conference of Seventh-day Adventists*

"Pastor Pavel Goia passionately shares powerful true stories which are pleasantly instructive on practical aspects of prayer. This book will transform the prayer life of any reader earnestly seeking to experience a meaningful personal relationship with God. A delightfully easy and captivating reading, loaded with solid practical prayer principles presented in a simple, inspiring, and convincing manner. Indeed, a necessary reading for any earnest seeker for God."

Geoffrey G. Mbwana, *General Vice President, General Conference of Seventh-day Adventists*

"One of the greatest needs of a Christian living in the 21st century is to be constantly aware and conscious of the reality of God's presence. God is real! He is at work! Prayers are answered, and miracles are happening even today! The life experiences of Pastor Pavel Goia presented in this book underscore this point. I am sure the readers of this book will be blessed and encouraged to live daily in God's presence!"

Artur A. Stele, *General Vice President, General Conference of Seventh-day Adventists*

"From the first chapter, it is very apparent that this is a practical, how-to book, which is backed up by inspirational examples from Pavel Goia's experience. Once I started reading, I couldn't put it down. In simple but not simplistic ways, he explains how to have a more spirit-filled and dynamic prayer life. Don't read this book unless you are prepared to be changed."

Audrey Andersson, *Executive Secretary, Trans-European Divison of Seventh-day Adventists*

"If you long for a closer relationship with God through prayer, inspiration for your daily walk, and a hunger for the Spirit, read this book. IN THE SPIRIT AND POWER: GOD'S PRESENCE AND ANSWERS TO PRAYER IN PAVEL GOIA'S JOURNEY is an extraordinary book with personal stories and practical applications leading the reader to a real experience with the Lord. It is a book you will read more than once and one you will want to share with your friends."

Jonas and **Raquel Arrais**, *Ministerial, Children's, Family, and Women's Ministries, Northern Asia-Pacific Division*

"My heart was thrilled, and my faith was dependent as I was reading IN THE SPIRIT AND POWER by Pavel Goia. I saw an amazing God who is present today in the world and love and cares about His children. He is all powerful and yet all loving. If you want to go deeper in your love for God or want to restore your first love for Him, this book is a must read for you."

S. Joseph Kidder, *Professor of Applied Theology and Discipleship at the Seventh-day Adventist Theological Seminary at Andrews University*

"If you think miracles ended with the book of Acts . . . and prayer doesn't really make that big a difference . . . do not read this book. But if you're ready for God to "do a new thing" in your life, your church, your world—you can't afford not to read it. Trust me—you'll never be the same again."

Dwight K. Nelson, *Lead Pastor, Pioneer Memorial Church, Berrien Springs, Michigan*

"Thank God for Pavel Goia's two fathers—earthly and heavenly. They taught him, 'Pray today. Study today. Surrender today. Serve today.' This is not just another book on prayer. This is not about prideful holiness; it is about sacrificial service. Pavel says, 'Ask so you can give'—and watch it change your life."

Jeffrey O. Brown, *Associate Ministerial Secretary, General Conference Ministerial Association*

"This is not just another book. It is the captivating and inspiring journey of a life of prayer and faith that leads us by the hand down trails of miracles and compels us to trust in the God of the impossible, the God of miracles, and the God of new beginnings."

Robert Costa, *Associate Ministerial Secretary, Evangelism and Church Growth, General Conference Ministerial Association*

"Emerging from a cold and godless communist Romania comes Pavel Goia, with amazing stories from a remarkable life of prayer. Ably assisted by Kelly Mowrer, Dr. Goia reveals the reality of the true God of heaven, who answers sincere prayers of the heart, even in the most hostile circumstances. Readers are left wanting more—more stories and their own similar experience with the loving God of the universe."

Anthony R. Kent, *Associate Ministerial Secretary, General Conference Ministerial Association*

"Everyone who longs for Holy Spirit power in their prayer life needs to read THIS book. The miracle stories are gripping, but the heart lessons shared throughout the testimonies are what really bring Pavel's message home with relevance and clarity. This book is challenging ME in my need for deeper prayer and greater faith. I will be sharing this book with many!"

Melody Mason, author of *Daring to Ask for More*

"Jesus calls each of us to experience the same amazing spiritual transformation and miracles as the early church believers. For years, our family has seen Pavel and Daniela Goia living this kind of authentic Spirit-powered adventure. Reading their stories and life lessons is like discovering a new present-day chapter of the book of Acts! If you seek a joyful, victorious walk of grace, read this book and let God change you, your family, your church, and the world by His power!"

Jerry and **Janet Page**, *Ministerial Secretary and Associate Ministerial Secretary, General Conference Ministerial Association*

ACKNOWLEDGMENTS

First, all my thankfulness and praise go to **God** for His infinite love expressed through Jesus, and for His presence with me every moment through the Holy Spirit.

Next, to my beloved wife, **Daniela**. I'm so grateful to God for you and for how He has blessed our family.

To my mom and dad, **Pavel** and **Eugenia**—I will continue to thank them throughout eternity because they taught me to know and love God.

To my co-author, **Kelly Mowrer**, with my whole heart, I give profound appreciation for her committed prayers, vision, and support of this book. She worked hard, she was patient, and she was flexible. It was a blessing to work with her.

To Pastor **Jerry Page** for his prayerful leadership and help in this project. At every step, every obstacle, he worked according to his prayers, and the Spirit answered with power.

To **Sheryl Beck** for her skillful editing, outstanding organization, wisdom, reliability, kindness, and patience.

To **Estrellita Jiménez** and **Tatiana Patrasco** for their generous gift of time in transcribing many sermons. These documents were invaluable in the writing of this manuscript.

To **Mario Martinelli** and the team at Safeliz Publishing for their mission-minded guidance, sacrificial diligence, and unending patience.

To my dedicated **colleagues in ministry** and my wonderful **church members**, too numerous to name. Thank you for your friendship and service to God through the years.

There are three people who deserve special mention for reasons which will become clear in the book:

Thank you to Pastor **Traian** and his wife, **Irina**, who invested time and love into a generation of youth who still walk with God because of their ministry; and

To **Pitzi**—my friend to this day.

To God be all the glory.

ACKNOWLEDGMENTS

CONTENTS

INTRODUCTION

NO LONGER HUNGRY

"But you shall receive power when the Holy Spirit has come upon you; and you shall be witnesses to Me in Jerusalem, and in all Judea and Samaria, and to the end of the earth."
Acts 1:8

The wind was frigid. My wife, Daniela, and I stood waiting in a long line behind an apartment building on the Andrews University campus in Michigan. An older gentleman, Mr. Tricket, provided canned food for the students needing it. The snow was high, and our shoes and socks were soaking wet. We were freezing and dizzy with hunger because we had not eaten for the last five days. Every piece of food we had was for our children.

Daniela and I learned how to fast—by necessity. My wife can fast for a long time. Even two weeks. I can fast, also. But never more than five hours at a time. This time I did it for five days. Now that we got a few cans of green beans, we went back to our apartment.

Tuition and books were expensive, not to mention housing, insurance, food, clothing, utilities, schooling for our two boys, and many more. Daniela held two jobs but was only paid $6 an hour. I also worked two jobs and carried a heavy academic load because I was trying to pack three years of schooling into one and a half.

We had arrived in America from our native Romania only two years earlier. I was still learning the English language while studying Greek and Hebrew from English-speaking professors, plus taking many other classes. By God's grace, I got good grades. However, regardless of how much we prayed or worked, we still struggled. We told absolutely no one about it—we just kept praying and working harder.

Then things got worse. We received a letter from school housing that we would be evicted if we didn't pay our rent by the end of the week. And we got a letter from the school that I could not register for the next semester unless we paid the tuition in full.

I fervently prayed, over and over, that God would intervene. But nothing happened. I didn't understand and even felt upset with God! Have you ever prayed yet don't seem to get any answer or relief? Do you carry heavy burdens to God in prayer and walk away still carrying those burdens?

Daniela and I have been there. The more we talked and thought about it, the more discouraged and depressed we were. The more we looked for answers to our problems, the more the problems multiplied. Tired, disheartened, and hungry, we went to bed. It seemed to me there was nothing else we could do. We felt powerless about all these things.

Do Not Forget

The following day, we read from Deuteronomy 4 during our devotional. We both sensed this Bible story was specifically speaking to us. It was where God told Moses to write down all the things He did for the children of Israel and read these stories to their children and grandchildren again and again, so they would never forget how God led them.

Next, we read from another inspired book, and our eyes stopped over this powerful passage: "We have nothing to fear for the future except as we shall forget the way the Lord has led us, and His teaching in our past history."[1]

We both were quiet for a few moments listening to the Holy Spirit in our thoughts. Then we started talking together. We decided to stop focusing on our trials. Instead, we would turn our focus on Jesus, His love, His promises, and the amazing ways He had already led us. We started to recall some of the stories of His intervention in our lives. The more we talked, the more peace and courage we received.

There were a few of my classmates who were facing even greater challenges. One lost his wife to cancer. Another one lost both his parents in a car accident. Altogether, we remembered seven other classmates and their families who were struggling. So we went to share some Bible promises and prayed with them.

After we visited each of them and returned home, *our* prayers were transformed, and we were no longer hungry for physical food. Instead of asking for food or help, we prayed for God to fill us with His Holy Spirit. We prayed for fresh oil—fresh anointing. We asked Him to baptize us every morning and make us like Jesus so that we would be a blessing to others.

We still placed our needs before Him, but we also thanked Him for His many other provisions, expressing our faith that He would continue to care for us. Then we spent the rest of our prayer presenting the families we had just visited, asking for God's intervention in their lives. For the first time in many days, we felt peace—real peace.

That night, a man we had never seen before knocked on our door looking for the couple who previously lived in the apartment. When he found out they had moved, he was disappointed. "Oh no. My jacket needs fixing, and the wife always fixed my clothing."

"Well," I answered, "we used to have a small business making clothing. My wife can fix it in no time."

"Great! Here it is. I am going to give you $20 right away for the work, and I will wait in the car."

Daniela started to fix the jacket. I could not wait any longer to eat, so I took his payment and ran to the grocery store. With the food in my hands, I walked and ate with a big smile on my face.

The man was still waiting and noticed me enjoying my food. "You must have been very hungry to run to the store right away," he said. "God has really blessed my farm. I have my trunk full of produce. Can you use it?"

"Yes," I stammered in shock. "That would be a tremendous blessing!"

He opened his trunk, and I saw heaven right there. Eight big boxes of produce, plus a box of bread from his bakery. Those nine boxes filled our tiny living room! I had tears in my eyes.

We thanked the man as he left, then hugged each other and dropped to our knees. After praising God, I wanted to continue eating right away, but Daniela stopped me.

"We will not touch it yet," she said. "Let's divide everything into eight equal boxes, then take one to each of your classmates we visited this afternoon. We will keep only one for ourselves."

That was difficult for me, but I knew she was right. And so I agreed. We visited each of the seven families and shared a box of food with them. We saw the tears of joy in their eyes. While we wanted to bless them, we seemed to get the greatest blessing.

We got back home, ate, praised God, and went to sleep. The next day, our friend from Tennessee called and asked how we were doing. "In the last few weeks, you don't seem as talkative as you usually are. Is something wrong?"

Not wanting to complain, I said, "No, all is good."

He didn't believe me. He called the housing department and found out that we were behind with rent. He paid the past due amount—plus three months in advance!

I then went to the school to plead my case, asking if I could pay the tuition after the summer. They said, "No need. Your tuition was paid in full for the entire year by an anonymous person who wanted to pass on God's blessings to others."

I got back to our apartment and checked the mailbox. Inside was an envelope of cash—the exact amount we owed the electric company. We were speechless. We had not told anyone about our challenges, let alone the very amount we owed!

God went above and beyond whatever we could have imagined. We decided to write down these stories and share them with our kids and friends because they showed not only His amazing love but also the way He works. They also reveal what He desires from us today.

God calls us to put aside ourselves and pray for the Holy Spirit so that we may truly know Him. The more we know Him, the more we love Him, and the more we trust Him. As we get closer to Him, He gets closer to us until we become one. He lives in us.

Only when we experience Him through His Spirit will we have something to share. Only then can we help others know Him, too. When people see Jesus in us, then we are truly Christians. His presence in us touches hearts in ways that we can never do on our own.

What Questions Do You Have?

As I travel, people often ask me these questions:

How can I know God better? How can I be filled with the Holy Spirit? Can I really have the assurance that I am saved?

How do I find His plans for me? How can I be led by His Spirit?

What can I expect when I pray? Why does God take so long to answer me?

How can I experience His transforming power in my life and my church? When will the Holy Spirit come as we read about in the book of Acts?

These wonderful gifts are promised in the Bible—they are secure. But they often don't happen the way we would imagine or expect. God's plans are far beyond our human plans, and God's wisdom doesn't always make sense to our human minds.

When God works, things may even seem to go in the *wrong* direction. He told Joseph that he would be put over his family, but Joseph was sold as a slave and put in prison. God told Moses that he would deliver Israel. But then Moses had to run into the wilderness for forty long years.

Before God can use us, He sometimes allows trials to teach us to follow *His* plans and trust *His* wisdom—not our own.

But how do we do that? How do we even know God and His plans? How do we distinguish His voice? How do we experience His power, His transforming love, and His salvation? How do we help those around us to know Him? How do we grow—and how does our church grow?

This book doesn't pretend to give exhaustive or theological answers to all these questions. But in sharing my stories, both from childhood and throughout my years of ministry, I hope you will find some practical insights and answers to these questions.

I even share key thoughts more than once because they are especially important in my life. I believe that the more we repeat them and dwell on them, the more we understand them and apply them.

God has never changed.

The same God who talked to Moses and Abraham, John and Peter, wants to communicate with *you* today. He has plans for *you*!

He who transformed Paul from a persecutor to an apostle wants to give you, me, and all His children this same transforming power today.

All around the world, I see Christians nearly bursting with their desire to have a closer relationship with Jesus, to know Him, and serve Him. I see a hunger for spiritual growth, a hunger for revival. We sense Jesus calling us to a deeper experience through His Holy Spirit.

We long for a personal walk with Him where we hear and know His voice.

When Daniela and I reached our lowest point years ago, God opened our hearts. He called us to change our focus. Instead of hungering to resolve our physical needs, we must hunger for *His* presence, for *His* Spirit.

Today, He's calling you and me and His entire church to put ourselves aside and seek the Holy Spirit so that we may go as witnesses to the world—witnesses who show Christ through their self-sacrifice and love and live His promises in every trial.

"There is no limit to the usefulness of one who, putting self aside, makes room for the working of the Holy Spirit upon his heart and lives a life wholly consecrated to God."[2]

When the Holy Spirit comes, He transforms us. Our lives become a fragrance, a light, a blessing.

I pray this book will draw you into a closer relationship with God and help you know Him more in a real way. Jesus is coming soon! There is no more time to lose. We must start now! If we give Him permission today, the Spirit can move us into this powerful experience.

Pavel Goia

Important Note: All the stories in this book are true. Some names and key details have been disguised to ensure privacy.

[1] Ellen G. White, *Testimonies to Ministers and Gospel Workers*, 31.

[2] Ellen G. White, *Ministry of Healing*, 159.

CHAPTER 1

FIND A DIFFERENT GOD

I was nineteen years old and facing the biggest crisis of my life. I was about to be expelled from the University of Bucharest because I would not attend classes on Sabbath.

My thoughts raced. During those years in Communist Romania, people without education lived difficult lives. Even getting into the university in the first place had been nearly impossible. When I applied, 976 students were competing for ten seats. I scored fourth in the testing and was very happy because now I could have a good life—a comfortable, decent life.

Then pressure began building as I missed Saturday classes week after week. I desperately prayed that God would help me. But I received no answer.

One day, the president of the university gave me an ultimatum.

"Goia, if you go to church, you have no future in this country. We will expel you from school and that will be the end of your education. This coming Saturday is your last chance. If you come to school, you are in. If you don't come, you are out. Your choice."

Sabbath was getting closer, and my internal conflict grew worse. My stomach tensed up so much that I couldn't eat. I'd lay awake at night wondering why God didn't answer my prayers. Then I'd pray even more urgently. The choice felt unbearable.

In despair, I called my father and poured everything out to him. "Dad, I don't know what else to do. I've tried to talk to them. I've prayed for hours. I've fasted. I've claimed His promises. I even had faith. Shouldn't I get an answer if I have faith? If I don't go to school this coming Sabbath, I will be expelled and lose everything. Tell me what more I need to do so that He will answer my prayer."

Dad paused. "Son," he finally answered, "you need to find a different god."

My mind went blank. "What do you mean?"

"You think God is there to grant your wishes, but He is the master, and you are His servant. You must focus on Him instead of focusing on school."

I still didn't understand. "How do you want me to pray?" I asked.

"You want God to save your schooling and your future. But you are not the center of the universe—Jesus is. When you pray, say, 'Lord, I would like You to save my education; nevertheless, please do what honors *You*. If my presence in this school serves You, let me be there and be a light for You. If not, take me from there and put me wherever honors and serves You.' When you give up self and put God in the center, when you fully surrender everything, when you are willing to sacrifice everything, including school, that is the prayer that He answers.

"Switch your prayer, son. Then you will experience power. Whatever you try to save, you will lose. But whatever you are willing to lose, surrender, and give to Him, that's what you save. That is what He can protect, preserve, use, and bless.

"You may think that school is what you need—which is why you pray about it. But your real need is to know God—to know His will. You need a relationship with Him. You need to know Him and trust in Him *more* than you need school. Son, you cannot have it all—God and school, or whatever else. God may allow you to stay in school or not, but that should not be your concern. You need to choose who comes first. You may say, 'God comes first.' But then you struggle in prayer to surrender school, which makes it clear that school comes first. Whatever you cannot surrender, whatever comes first—that's what you worship. You cannot worship God and other things at the same time. You cannot compromise. You need to choose. You cannot have a divided heart. Either all for God or nothing."

Why Don't We See Power?

Now let me pause my story and ask you a question.

Why don't we see power in our lives or the church today?

We've been Christians for years, for decades sometimes, and we still lack power. We're busy with projects, programs, and church activities, which are good and necessary. But we know that there is something vital missing in our lives and the church. We desire more.

We talk so much about Jesus, His love, His power, and what He has done in the past—but there is not much that happens in our lives, our families, and our churches. We talk about the book of Acts: the Pentecost, the miracles, the conversions, the incredible growth, and all that happened then. We desire it today. But how can it happen all over again? We're facing challenging times, and we don't know what to do.

Around the world, the prophecies we have learned since we were children are fulfilling before our eyes. Politically, economically, religiously, and in all other ways, things are happening in preparation for Jesus' coming—not in the far future, but extremely soon.

We need God now more than ever before. We need to finish the work. We need to get ready for the greatest crisis in history. We need to be ready for His second coming. And for that, we need His presence and power. But how do we receive power?

Jesus told the disciples to *pray until* they receive the Holy Spirit. And He said that when the Holy Spirit comes, they shall receive power (Acts 1:8). Then they were to go and preach the good news.

Before sending them out, Jesus first asked them to stay, wait, and pray. He didn't ask them to pray just once, twice, or for a week, or forty days. The Great Commission does not begin with going to the whole world and telling the good news. *First*, we must wait and pray. Pray for the power of the Holy Spirit. Jesus said, *pray until* . . . He was clear. *Pray UNTIL you receive the Holy Spirit. Then you shall receive power.*

When the Holy Spirit came at Pentecost, the disciples began to truly understand Jesus' sacrifice, to grasp the prophecies and the great controversy. The coming of the Spirit transformed them and the whole known world through them. They forgot themselves and focused entirely on God and His mission. This outpouring of the Holy Spirit was symbolized as the early rain.

Today, we also are to *pray until* we receive the Holy Spirit, which will be the latter rain. Zechariah 10:1 says, "Ask the LORD for rain in the time of the latter rain."

Now is the time of the latter rain.
We need to pray for it.

As individuals and as a church, how can we grow spiritually if we don't have spiritual power? Spiritual power only comes when the Holy Spirit comes. And the Holy Spirit comes when we pray.

We cannot fight spiritual battles in human power. For spiritual war, we need spiritual power. Human wisdom, plans, and strategies may be good, but they will never bear real success without the power of the Holy Spirit. We can plant the seeds, water, till, and weed, but only God gives the growth. This work is not done in human strength "'but by My Spirit,' says the LORD of hosts" (Zech. 4:6).

Jesus told the disciples clearly that it was better if He went because He would then send them the Comforter (John 16:7). And He told them that the Holy Spirit would lead them and help them in *all* things and into *all* truth (John 16:13). *Everything* is possible through His Spirit; *nothing* is possible in our own power. In His Spirit are concentrated *all* heavenly resources.

The disciples prayed together in one accord. They prayed for the promised Comforter. And when they prayed, they received the Holy Spirit. And when they received the Holy Spirit, they received power. And then everything else happened in ways that they could have never done or imagined. A small group of persecuted people with no money, media, or influence turned the world upside down.

Are we ready to pray until we receive the power of the Holy Spirit today?

My father used to say, "I don't pray for what I *think* I need because I'm not sure I know what is best to ask for. I pray for what God wants me to pray for—His will, plan, and honor. And I pray until I am filled with His presence! I pray until the Holy Spirit takes control over me, my mind, words, and my actions. Then God can change me, grow me, inspire me, lead me and use me. Only God's presence in me can bring real results. I no longer focus on self but rather on Him."

God can never work in us or use us until we make His presence and plans our priority. We need to seek His presence and be filled with His Spirit.

Christ wants to live in us through the Holy Spirit.
He wants to fill us with His Spirit
—to pour His power into us.

Wow. That's a big concept. How can this happen in our lives? In our churches?

The Rest of the Story

Back to my story about school.

Oh, how I struggled! Of course, I wanted to obey God—but what I *really* wanted was for Him to fix it so I didn't have to choose. I wanted to *say* I surrendered my school, yet I didn't want to give up my entire future career.

But my dad was right—I needed to change my prayer. I was even more convicted when I read my devotional book: "When we pray, we need to trust God with the outcome; we need to allow Him to work as He sees best."

God doesn't work with half-committed people.

Still, it felt like pulling teeth to get the words out.

"Lord, You already know how I hate to say these words. You know that I don't want to lose my education and ruin my future. But if you really think that I should not be in school, I give You my consent to do what You want. You know my heart, Lord, I am sorry."

Then my heart and prayer began to change. "Do what would honor and serve You. Help me make You a priority, seek Your will more than my will, and seek a relationship with You above all other things." On and on, my words poured out.

The moment I was willing to give up my career and commit everything to God, forgetting myself, the crushing weight of despair dropped away. I felt a peace like I'd never experienced before in my life. In fact, I felt that God was right there next to me. I was afraid even to open my eyes or keep talking. What could I have said in His presence? I decided to trust in Him. At that moment, a Romanian song came to my mind, "The one that trusts in the Lord has no worries."

On Thursday, I went to school, determined to keep Sabbath at any cost and no longer concerned with the outcome. Mrs. Radu, the school secretary, greeted me and began asking questions. During our long conversation, she said, "Pavel, you are a good student. It is a pity to lose your education. Come to school, and you can pray in your mind."

"I will not compromise, Mrs. Radu. God comes first, second, and in every place in my life. If God wants to save my education, He can do it, and He will do it. But if He doesn't intervene, why would I even want to be in school?"

"You are a fanatic! Goia, there is no God. Have you seen Him?"

"Yes, last night in prayer."

She shook her head in disbelief. "You really have lost your mind," she said. "Wake up! No god can save you from the government."

"Mrs. Radu, my God is bigger than *any* government. And *He* is my priority, not school."

"Well," she said, turning away, "I want to see what god can save you from a communist government."

I prayed again that night, but I was no longer pleading for my education or future. Instead, I asked God to do whatever was necessary for Mrs. Radu and the school to know Him.

"Lord, please help them know that there is a real God who loves them—a God who is coming soon and who wants to save them."

Friday was supposed to be my last day of classes before being expelled. I didn't know what to expect as I approached the school for the final time. The first person I saw was Mrs. Radu. As soon as she saw me, she came running. She was so pale and shaken that I thought she was sick.

"Pavel, do you know anyone in the government?"

"No," I replied. "Why do you ask?"

"Do you know anyone in the Central Committee?"

"No."

"Do you know Ceausescu?"

"Well, everyone knows the president of the country. I see him on TV."

"No, no, no. Are you relatives or close friends?"

"Me and the president? Ha, ha!" I was smiling. I thought she was kidding.

"Are you *positive* you are being honest with me?" she asked again.

Now I was beginning to feel puzzled. "Yes, Mrs. Radu, I am being totally honest. All I know about the government is that there are thousands of roses in front of the government palace. Sometimes I stop by and take a free rose from there for my wife, Daniela. That's all the government I know."

She just stared at me in disbelief, shaking her head a little. "Then there is a God!" she said, almost to herself. "Pavel, for twenty-one years, I have worked at this university. Never have I seen the government take an action like this! This morning, the president spoke on TV. To help the ailing economy by conserving energy, he canceled all Saturday classes for the entire country, effective today. If this law had come on Monday rather than today, you would have been expelled from school for the rest of your life. No one could have saved you."

Then her voice lowered. "There must be a God after all," she almost whispered. "Your God is real, and He loves you!"

I answered, "Mrs. Radu, yes, my God is real, and He loves me. He gave His Son for you and for me. But when I prayed just for me, He did not answer. When I gave up self and prayed for whatever best served Him and that more people, like you, may know Him, then He worked in a way that I could have never imagined."

Why Don't We Have Power When We Pray Today?

As my father said long ago, we are praying the wrong prayers. We forget to fix our eyes on God and instead fix our eyes on self, other people, problems, needs, challenges, and all types of things. We're praying *more* for answers, blessings, help, or even church growth and *less* for God's presence and will. God longs to give us Himself most of all. We often have made the things God intended as blessings into idols and have transformed them into curses. We seek His help instead of His presence, which we really need most. We need to be filled with Him.

We often worship the blessings of God instead of the God of the blessings.

How can any blessing help us if we miss God's presence? If we miss a deep relationship with Him? A total dependence on Him?

Jesus said to ask, seek, knock—for the gift of the Holy Spirit. Our Father in heaven is looking for people who thirst for Him, who desire Him more than anything else. People who forget self and make Him the center. People who seek His presence and His leading. He promised to give His Holy Spirit to those who ask (Luke 11:13).

He will help us seek Him, desire Him, know Him, and love Him above all else.

SUMMARY

Jesus told the disciples to *pray until* they received the Holy Spirit. Only when the Holy Spirit came upon them did they receive power. Only after that were they to go and preach the good news.

Think what power will flow in our lives, what power will flow in our church, when God becomes the center of our prayers—when we *pray until* the Holy Spirit fills us, leads us, controls us, and speaks through us all for the glory of our Father!

2 CHAPTER

DON'T LOOK FOR A MIRACLE

I was named after my father, Pavel Goia—although no one called me Pavel while I was growing up. My grandmother called me Pavelucu, which got shortened to Lucu (*Lū-kū*), and then *everyone* called me Lucu.

I grew up in communist Romania. When I was in fifth grade, my father was called to the local police station and threatened with death for being a significant part of a new church building project.

We'd been working for months in secret every night. We used no lights—only the moon. I still have a scar on my chest from hitting a two-by-four as I jumped from a piece of scaffolding.

We also used no power tools so there would be no noise. I remember the pastor's wife stirring concrete with a shovel by hand.

Most of our congregation worked together. Young, old, men, women, children.

The church board prayed for months before deciding to go ahead. They knew that they could be arrested. We were only permitted to worship in the old rundown building. We all knew the government wouldn't allow us to build a new church.

The communist party in Romania pretended to the outside world that they recognized religious freedom. In reality, there was *no* tolerance. Zero. Uncounted numbers of Christians were arrested and sent to prison for bringing religious books into the country or printing them, or refusing to work on Sabbath during military service. Some died from beatings or starvation.

People lived in fear. They were afraid to say the wrong thing. Afraid even to think.

Through the years, my father, and many other brave church members, risked *everything* to share their faith.

I remember him telling us, "Do not be afraid. We are sons and daughters of the King. Why would we be afraid of people? We have experienced the power of our God, and He is real. If God is for us, who can be against us? If we are afraid, we either have only a theory of God without God's presence, or we have a very small God. Our God is infinite in power and love and resources, and He is with us. We are never alone."

Our God is real.
Only those who do not have a real God
live in fear.

To hide our illegal construction, we left the front wall of the old church in place and built behind it. But once the new building became taller than the old front wall, someone reported us to the police.

They came late at night, pounding on the locked gate of our church property. "Open up!" they shouted, standing outside the fence. My father walked across the church yard—right up to the front gate with its beautiful almond tree on the left side and an apple tree on the right side.

"Open up *now*!" the leader yelled in his face.

"Do you have a warrant?" my father asked. He was completely relaxed and calm.

"No!"

"Then we will not open the gate," my father replied. "Go get the warrant, and then we will let you in."

The leader grew more furious. "It's too late at night," he shouted. "I cannot get a warrant at this time."

"Then wait until tomorrow," my father answered.

"You're going to pay for this!" the policeman screamed.

The Raid

I saw police yell at my father a few different times through the years. He also told us several more stories of when they called him to the police station. Whenever the authorities got wind of something they deemed subversive, they would descend on our house to search. Or they would summon him to police headquarters for interrogation.

As always, my father was courageous and wise as a result of his walk with Jesus. And this wisdom extended to all areas of his life. People listened when he talked. He was extremely diligent and enterprising and produced some honey. Also, he worked as a building contractor. His work was highly respected and was trusted by the local city officials for complex jobs.

My mother, Eugenia, was quiet and kind and made a wonderful home for us. She would teach me two or three Bible verses each morning until I knew them by memory. Every single day. She would also teach me songs—making sure I knew all stanzas. Most of all, she would tell Bible stories and emphasize their lessons. She taught me, with love and patience, to know God through His Word.

My parents raised my sisters and me to love God and love people. "God is with you," they would tell us. "You are never alone. Put your trust in Him. Keep your eyes on Him. Stay with Him."

I remember my father being a man of prayer. I would often slip out to the kitchen late at night to get something to eat and see him on his knees.

Once, I asked him, "Why do you pray so much?"

He said, "Son, I need to be filled with God's Spirit. Fully filled. If you really want to have success in your life—victory, growth, results—you need to spend time in prayer to get God's presence. Jesus said that the Comforter would lead us in all things. When you are filled by the Spirit, He leads you in all things better than you imagine or plan. When you get God and allow Him to lead you, you get everything. You need to make sure that you are so filled with His presence that you follow His plan and trust in Him." He would then say, "I also pray for you and your sisters and your mom and the church."

"But I don't need so much prayer," I replied once.

"That's why I pray so much for you," he answered.

Periodically, either my father or my mother would cross into former Yugoslavia to secretly bring back Bibles. Sometimes, a friend from Yugoslavia would come over and bring them. We all knew the authorities would impose the harshest punishment if they discovered any of this.

I remember one time when my father crossed the Danube and brought back boxes of smuggled Bibles—ten, twenty boxes. We stacked them in a large pile in the middle of our living room.

"I think we will be raided by *Securitatea* (*secure-i-ta-tea*) tonight," he told us.

Securitatea was the brutal secret police agency of dictator Nicolae Ceausescu, then leader of Romania. When they took people, harsh interrogations followed. Some were pushed to become informants, were beaten, and tortured. Some did not return home. People would shake with fear when they appeared. *Securitatea* was merciless.

"Why do you think we will be raided, Pavel?" my mom asked.

"Because I saw Brother Petru following me on his bike. He had no reason to be on the street where I was. He ducked out of sight when he realized that I noticed him."

Brother Petru and his wife were conservative, respected church members. They taught Sabbath School classes and helped in many ways. But even when I was very young, my father told me, "Lucu, I want you to be especially careful of what you say when you are around Brother Petru. *Be careful*," he emphasized.

My father suspected that Brother Petru was a police informant—a traitor. In those hard years, every congregation had quite a few spies—members who were secretly paid to tell authorities what went on.

Many of these informants thought that they had no choice. "You have two options," the police would tell them. "Either go to prison, get beaten, get tortured—or tell us what happens in church. And you'll be free."

On this particular night, we all knew that if the police came to our door, they would see the smuggled Bibles right away. There was nowhere to hide them.

But I wasn't very worried. By nature, I was confident and optimistic.

"We just need to pray and have faith," I told everyone.

My father smiled at me. "Let me ask you a question, Lucu," he said. "Why do you think Jesus asked us to have faith when we pray?"

"Well, because faith is what gets the answers to our prayers."

"That's what many people think," he said. "They believe that if they pray with enough faith, they will somehow twist God's arm so that He has no choice but to do what they want. They don't understand that using faith to get answers is like trying to manipulate God with our faith.

"Faith does not *force* God to give what we ask," he continued. "Instead, faith changes our hearts. With faith, no matter what happens, we believe He is in control and that whatever He does is best. Faith is not to change God but to change you. Faith helps you trust in Him when you don't understand what is going on. It keeps your eyes on Him and His promises."

Faith does not manipulate God.
Faith does not change God's will.
Faith changes us.
Even when we don't understand what is going on,
we still trust Him.

While we were talking, we heard footsteps in the hall outside our apartment, and then someone pounded on the door. "Open up!" a voice shouted.

My father crossed to the door and opened it. "Good evening," he said.

Three officers stood there. "We have received reports that you are smuggling Bibles. Do you have illegal Bibles in this house?"

I wondered what my father would say. He always told us never to lie. "Don't compromise the truth," he'd say, "because compromise won't save you. Tell the truth or just keep quiet. Always pray for wisdom to know what to answer. Jesus promised wisdom to those who ask."

Now my father answered the officer. "Tell me," he said, as though he was curious, "what is your job?"

The leader glared at him. "We are police officers."

"Well, then," my father continued with a slight smile, "it must be that *your* job as police officers is to search. I, of course, could not do your job by *telling* you if there are illegal Bibles here. But feel free to come inside and look. Then you will be doing your job. If *I* do your job, then I should probably get your salary."

I'd heard him say something similar before during another raid. In disgust, the leader turned away, saying, "He wouldn't be asking us to come in and search if he had Bibles. We're leaving."

But this time, the officer shoved my father out of the way and stomped in. The others followed him, crowding into our small living room. The large cartons of smuggled Bibles stood right in the center, taller than a man's waist. They absolutely dominated the room.

We all thought the next question was going to be, "What is in the boxes?" But instead, the leader told the officers to search the house. They started looking everywhere. Doors began slamming. "Check under the mattresses," came the order. "And in the closets. Every single possible place."

We could hear them yanking open all of the drawers. My mother had tears in her eyes. I knew she was praying. But my father stood relaxed. His eyes were filled with peace as they met mine.

Next, the police searched the kitchen, emptying cupboards and throwing things aside. Then back to the living room, where they looked behind every piece of furniture. They flipped chairs and tossed cushions to the floor.

Over and over, they walked past that giant stack of boxes in the middle of the living room. But they never stopped. They never stumbled into them, either. It was as if the pile was simply invisible to them.

Finally, one of them said, "We searched everywhere. Maybe our tip was wrong. Maybe they moved them somewhere else before we got here."

The leader stopped in front of my father. "I don't know where you have hidden the Bibles," he shouted, "but someday you will be caught. And you *will* be punished."

The Arrest

Now I will go back to the story of the night when my father refused to open the locked church gate unless the police got a warrant.

Even though they left because it was too late to get paperwork that night, we all knew they would return soon. My father and the other leaders urged our pastor to leave while he could. My father told the pastor, "You are young; you are committed. God still has a plan for you. Take your wife and go. Take a few days' vacation. Disappear—so that you don't get arrested."

"Uncle Goia," he answered, "what about you?"

"Don't worry. I have lived my life. I am older, and I am ready to retire. I can take being arrested."

The pastor left. When the police returned with the warrant, they demanded, "Who is the leader here?"

"I am," my father answered. "I am," another elder spoke up. "I am," said a third.

"You cannot all be leaders," the police shouted. "Who led the construction? We need to arrest somebody."

My father answered, "I am the one who was in charge of the construction. Arrest me."

They took my father to the police station for harsh interrogation. "We will demolish your church," they told him.

"Then we would have to worship in the marketplace, where all the city does their shopping and can listen to our service," my father replied.

Next, they threatened to arrest him and all others involved in the construction. The demands escalated. Stop building. Stop smuggling Bibles. Stop witnessing. "We don't have a god in our country," they screamed at my father. "There is no God. If you do not stop, we are going to terminate you right here."

My father answered, "God is my Master; I cannot stop. I do what He says. If I live, I live for Him. And if I die, it will feel like just a second to me until the resurrection. Then I will see Jesus. I do not care if I live or die."

The order to kill my father came directly from the mayor at city hall.

"Terminate him," he said on the phone. "You have my authorization. He will be a lesson for everybody else. Otherwise, these people will never stop. They believe their God is bigger than us. But they need to obey the government, not their God. So we will use him to teach them all a lesson."

The officer pushed his gun into my father's chest. "I will shoot you if you don't stop doing these things."

My father asked him to wait a moment and started to unbutton his shirt. The officer, confused, said, "Why would you unbutton it? The bullet goes through this shirt."

My father answered, "I know, but it would be such a pity to stain it. Better take it for someone poor. Then you can shoot me."

Everyone left except the officer who was to shoot him. "I'm sorry, Mr. Goia," he said, "but I have to follow the mayor's orders."

My father answered, "Let me pray first."

"There is no point in praying for mercy," the officer replied. "There is no God to save you."

"Oh, I'm not praying for mercy," my father answered, "I'm praying for *you*."

Then my father stood, put his arm around the officer, and prayed, "Lord, I want to see him in heaven. I don't mind dying. You died for me—I will joyfully die for You. It is a privilege. But Lord, would You use my death to save this man and his family? I want to see him in heaven."

After my father finished praying, he said, "Now I'm ready."

That very moment, the telephone rang. It was the chief of police.

"I just got a call from the mayor's deputy," he reported. "He says, 'Don't touch this man because the Spirit of the Living God is in him. After the mayor gave the execution order, he left city hall, and a drunk driver hit his car. The mayor is dead. If you touch this man, you fight God. Let him go home.' "

I will never forget my father coming home and saying, "They said to let me go because the Spirit of the Living God is in me."

The Last Test

We believe my father died because of the police a few years later. We don't know for sure, but many were silently terminated like this. I was about twenty-two years old at the time.

My father received a call to come to police headquarters for another interrogation. Uncounted times through the years, police would search our house or call him to come in.

"We got a tip," they would shout at him when he arrived. "People say you bring in Bibles. We believe you have them. You also duplicate religious books. You will pay if we catch you." On and on. Hours and hours of threats.

But they never caught him.

Because of his construction business, he was very well known in our area. During one interrogation, he heard them talking to each other. "If we kill him, we will make him a martyr. Everybody knows him in this city."

Now another summons. "Come down to headquarters for interrogation." Our whole family was praying when he went in. Just like we always did.

But he didn't come home that night.

We found out later that they barely interrogated him. Instead, they put him alone in a room. In the morning, two guys opened the door and allowed him to leave.

After a few days, his nose started to bleed. He went to a doctor who told him, "You have lymphatic leukemia. I believe that you may have been exposed to radiation. You have about three months to live."

We knew the communist government sometimes used radioactive poison to kill someone quietly. Although we have no clear proof of what exactly happened, this was a very strong possibility. He was almost sixty-two years old, strong, and in good health overwise.

Oh, how we prayed. My mother, my sisters, our pastor, and the whole church. My father started natural treatments right away. Apple juice. Carrot juice. Fresh vegetables.

Of course, I expected another miracle.

"Just keep praying," I told everyone. "God has performed so many miracles before—I know He's going to do it again."

But my father said, "Son, don't look for a miracle. Look for a relationship with Jesus. When you know Him, you don't need a miracle. When you know Him, you trust Him. Whatever happens, you say, 'I don't understand, but I know my Savior. I know that He loves me. I trust in Him and His decision. I am secure in His hand.' "

"But God answers the prayer of faith," I insisted.

"Yes, God honors our faith," he agreed. "But we must also remember that John the Baptist, Peter, Paul, and many others *suffered* for their faith. So why not us, too? Not every prayer brings deliverance from trials. And this is not about you or me. We are not the center. God is. Put God and His work first and let Him decide what is best. You see, Jesus came down and died for me. Can you understand that? He died for me! When I think about it, I am speechless, and I have no problem dying for Him. In fact, I consider it a privilege. If I live, I live for Him. If I die, I know I will see Him at the resurrection.

"Son," he continued, "it only takes a little faith to experience a miracle when we pray."

"Not to experience a miracle—that takes a* lot *of faith."

My father was a fighter and lived months longer than the doctor expected. I remember the doctor saying, "You have no defense. You have no immune system. Anything can kill you from now on. Anything—even the smallest flu."

A few months later, my father was moving beehive boxes out in the rain and caught pneumonia. At first, he was in the hospital, but soon there was nothing more to be done. We brought him back home to keep him comfortable.

As his body grew weaker, my father's faith and peace only grew stronger.

I asked him, "Why doesn't God answer my prayer to heal you?"

He again reminded me, "It is not about you or me. It is all about God. Don't put you or me in the center of prayer or the center of life. Forget self. Put God, His will, His honor, His service in the center. I shall decrease, and He shall increase (John 3:30). I don't focus on this life—I don't live for this life. My focus is Him, and I live for heaven. This life is short. I don't want this world. I want eternity with Him. And if heaven had eternity and streets of gold, but my Savior was not there, I wouldn't want heaven either. I just want to be with Him always.

"Jesus never promised comfort in this life. In fact, He says, 'In this life, you will have trials. But,' He also says, 'You are never alone. I will be with you always. Even when you go through waters, I will be with you.' "

"I know that," I said, "but He can still heal you."

"Son, forget self, focus on Him. Look around. We all think only about ourselves. All we do, talk about, and pray, is mostly about self. What if we all would forget self and just live for Him."

"But you have done so much for Him. Shouldn't He heal you? Then you could serve Him more?"

"I don't do things to get or deserve something. I do it because He lives in me, and I love Him. Remember, son, under big trees nothing grows. Sometimes you need to cut a big tree so smaller trees can develop. I pray that if I go, many others who didn't have the courage to serve God before would learn, and there would be 100 serving in my place. I pray that at my funeral people will focus on Him, not me. And more people will know Him and decide to serve Him. Son, Jesus is coming soon and that's my goal. That's what I am looking for."

I still couldn't process what he said. I could not accept it. I was praying non-stop for healing. I know we all were. He was not only my father—we were friends. I could talk to him openly about anything. He was always supportive. "Please God," I begged, "I cannot lose him."

But he took a turn for the worse. My mom, sisters, and I gathered around his bed.

I felt *so* frustrated with God. My father was a saint. *Why* wasn't God performing a miracle?

My sisters were paralyzed with grief. My mom was nearly sick herself and couldn't stop crying.

"Don't cry," my father told her, taking her hand. He looked at each of us. "Don't we have hope? Isn't that the difference between us and the world? I *know* I'm going to see Him. This is what you will say on my grave stone: 'I know that my Redeemer lives. My eyes are going to see Him face to face.' I have that confidence. I *will* see Him in the resurrection morning—and I will spend eternity with Him."

I desperately hung onto hope for a last-minute miracle. Standing there, we were all so devastated we could barely speak. Yet I still wanted everyone to pray.

Instead, my father said, "Let me pray for all of you."

Soon after he prayed, he fell into a coma. Then he was gone. Asleep in Jesus.

The Key

After my father died, I could not sleep at night. I could not eat. I could not pray.

I developed pressure in my heart and constant pain in my stomach. Day after day, week after week. The pain wouldn't leave.

By now you know that this book is not on the theory of prayer. I am writing from my heart. What I say about prayer, I am living myself. When my father died, I felt so desperate, so discouraged, so depressed, that I did not want to read the Bible. I did not want to pray. But I wanted to see my father again.

I remembered him saying to us as we stood around his bed, "When I will see Jesus face to face, I want my family to be there."

So, I made a conscious decision. I prayed each day, "Lord, I do not understand. I do not feel. But I am going to decide to trust in Your

Word. You are God. You are the Creator. You love me and You cannot lie. Lord, I trust Your promises." I would say that out loud.

I also read the Bible a lot, especially in the book of Job. In His mercy, God worked in my heart. The answer didn't come the way I wanted, nor in the timing I wanted. There was no great moment of deliverance.

But the more I prayed, the more I learned *how* to pray. The longer I prayed, the more time I spent with my Lord. The more time I spent with Him, the more I began to know Him.

And the more I began to know Him, the more I began to trust Him again.

Prayer connected me to God once more. And knowing God is our greatest need.

John 17:3 says, "Eternal life is to know you, the only true God" (CEV). In Greek, the word 'know' is *ginō´ skō*. This means "a heart relationship."

God wants a relationship with us. We don't have a relationship with someone unless we spend time with them.

That's why we pray. Not to get miracles, or deliverance, or answers, but to get God Himself.

Of course, He invites us to ask Him for all that we need. But prayer should be so much more than solving problems.

Prayer is not an activity.
Prayer is not only a conversation.
Prayer is connecting
with the God of the universe,
the King of Kings,
the Creator.

Prayer is not about getting answers or help but about getting God. Prayer is to know Him, love Him, trust Him, and follow Him to the degree that you forget self and He becomes everything in your life. Relationship with Him becomes the priority and focus of everything you do. You have one desire alone: to know Him, see Him, walk with Him, and be with Him. You pray, study the Word, and go to church, not as a duty, not because it's the right thing to do, but because you want to know Him and be with Him. You want Him more than you want help, blessings, or life.

Jesus is coming soon. I believe He is calling us to a complete change of our mindset on how to pray and how to do church.

It's so easy to keep the Sabbath, eat healthy food, and obey the doctrines. Those are all good and necessary things. But how much are we willing to make Jesus our highest priority? To put Him first above everything. To know Him and love Him to the degree that we say, like Paul, "I consider everything a loss because of the surpassing worth of knowing Jesus Christ my Lord" (Phil. 3:8, NIV).

We say that we long for the Holy Spirit. But if we really want our prayers filled with power, we must become connected to God by spending time with Him. Power only flows through connection. We must walk with Him like Enoch. Like Moses. Like Abraham.

The key to powerful prayer is being connected to God. Christianity isn't about the right theories or doing good things. Christianity is about the One to whom we are connected.

SUMMARY

Prayer connects us to God.

What a privilege it is to come into His presence and talk with Him openly.

The key to powerful prayer is seeking Him first—above all else. Our greatest need is not miracles, help, nor deliverance. Our greatest need is be filled with His Spirit. To be in Him, and He in us.

To know God is to have an intimate personal relationship by spending time in prayer seeking *Him*. The function of prayer is not to get answers but to have a relationship. To be connected. To experience His presence continually.

CHAPTER 3

THIS IS WAR

When I was in college in Bucharest many years ago, my best friend, Pitzi, and I attended a large church. The people were very friendly, and the church had good musical programs.

But the pastor was very old. I don't remember, maybe 87, 90, 110 years. I'm exaggerating a little to make a point.

He was a good man who served Jesus faithfully his whole life. But now, he was so old that he could hardly work or talk. Leaning on the pulpit, hardly breathing: "Brothers," he'd sort of gasp. And then he preached slowly. Very slowly. He'd stop to take deep breaths. Some in the congregation fell asleep. The youth on the balcony looked at magazines and told jokes.

"This church needs more life," I told Pitzi. "There's a great choir and nice musical programs, but we need more. There are no seminars to help spiritual growth, no Pathfinders, no evangelism, no community outreach, no Bible studies."

"Yes, but what can we do about it?" he answered. "We're just two students. Nobody knows us except the choir members and the youth we play soccer with at the park."

Pitzi was very practical. Also, very tall and funny. We'd known each other our whole lives.

"Well," I said, "we can do one of three things. Either we can complain or do nothing and just ignore it, or we can do what we both learned from our dads. They always tell us that the secret of church revival, the secret of growth, the secret of power—is prayer!"

"I do believe in prayer," Pitzi said, "but how can it help now?"

"That's why we pray," I said. "Number one, for God's intervention. Number two, for wisdom to know if we can do something."

"Ok," he agreed. "Do you plan to call the whole youth to pray with us?"

"No," I said. "If we call them, some would probably come out of curiosity but wouldn't be committed. Soon half would leave, and the other half would get discouraged, and we would lose everybody. Let's start small—just you and me. God doesn't despise small beginnings. Better to start small and grow than the other way."

"I like that," Pitzi said.

So Pitzi and I began to pray together.

Every revival in history
has started with one or two people praying.

When we prayed, we didn't say, "God, bless the church. Help the church grow." Or "Lord, we have this plan—bless our plans."

Instead, we said, "Lord, we need Your advice and leading. We need revival for ourselves; we need revival for our church. And we don't have a plan, and we don't have a strategy; we don't have a project, and we don't have any influence, wisdom, or power to do it ourselves. All we know is that nothing would work without You. So we ask for Your plan, and we ask for Your help."

In the Bible, all big stories happened by God's power alone. All people of faith have been people of prayer. They walked with God, communicated with God, and depended on God. God led them and worked through them.

For instance, the disciples prayed for the promise of the Holy Spirit. And when the Holy Spirit came, everything changed. The Holy Spirit did things through His power that the disciples would never have been able to accomplish on their own.

So Pitzi and I decided to pray. And we prayed for weeks. And months.

And absolutely *nothing* happened.

Why would God want us to pray for so long? Why wouldn't He just answer from the first prayer?

Answer to prayer is a process, not an event.

I believe the number one reason we need to persist in prayer is that God has to prepare us and those around us for the answer. It takes a while for God to work with us so that our mind is prepared for what He's about to ask or do.

Did you know that the great majority of prayers in the Bible were answered over time and not right away? Think about it.

Abraham waited twenty-five years after God promised him offspring before he had a child.

Joseph waited ten years as an enslaved person and three more in prison before being set free.

Moses waited forty years in the wilderness.

Daniel prayed for three weeks until he got an answer. The angel Gabriel told him, "The moment you began praying, a command was given. And now I am here to tell you what it was, for you are very precious to God. Listen carefully so that you can understand the meaning of your vision" (Dan. 9:23, NLT). While he was praying and waiting, God was actually fighting the evil forces that opposed any progress in God's plan and work. It is war; it is the great controversy (Dan. 10:12-14).

He Is Working

When you start praying, God starts working. You may not see it or be aware of what He is doing. Therefore, you may be tempted to think He does not answer. But He is always moving. When everything is ready, you *may* finally see the answer. Other times, you won't know the outcome until heaven. But He has been working on it all this time. Therefore, keep praying, so God keeps working.

Pitzi and I said to each other, "We will pray *until* we get an answer." The keyword was *until*.

How long should we pray? Until we get an answer.

Once a week, we prayed. Eventually, our friends began to notice. "Hey, what are you doing? You've met for a few weeks now. Do you go out and eat?"

"No, we pray."

"Really? How is that fun?" We didn't try to convince them about the need for prayer. My dad always told me that people usually only want what they cannot have. Someone with straight hair wants curly hair and the other way around. If you call someone to go on a mission trip, they have excuses. But if you tell them it is very exclusive, and perhaps they cannot come, then they would really want to go. People don't value things that come easy.

So, when people asked us, we said, "This is just a small prayer group. We are not inviting anyone else."

"But we are friends. Come on. You always invite us to do stuff together."

"Yes, but not this time. We prefer you don't come."

And word started to get around. "Pitzi and Lucu—those two guys who always play pranks—they have a very exclusive prayer group now."

More kids started asking about it. "What are you praying for?"

"We are praying for God to bring revival to our hearts and the church."

One girl, who was a gifted pianist, said, "Yes! I would like to see some change in the church—some revival! Can I come?" And she told others who then wanted to come.

So, we said, "OK, but there are rules. If you come, you've got to pray. You cannot joke and play around."

"Oh, you have rules? We don't like that."

"Then don't come."

"Okay, we accept the rules."

"And if you miss a meeting, you pay a fine—to the youth group fund. Or you pay for the ice cream when we go out Saturday nights. And you have to bring a cookie for everyone."

"Okay!"

Eventually, we had ten people. Then twenty. Every morning, everyone prayed alone in their homes at a specified time. Once a week, Friday night, we'd get together for half an hour of prayer and then half an hour of Bible study.

The more we prayed, the more we warmed up to prayer. The group kept growing. We moved the meeting to the church because there was no room anywhere else.

By now, we were investing so much time and energy in praying for people and their salvation that we actually *cared* about them. We wanted to do things for them. So we started to plan together.

The more we pray for somebody, the more we grow to love them.

"Let's go to the elderly of the church and clean their homes, do their grocery shopping, split their wood, and help them build their fire." "Let's go do Bible studies." "Let's go on a mission trip." "Let's go camping in the mountains." Let's go . . . Let's do . . . for the church!

The youth in that church became so committed and energized.

There was growth, and we all could see it. Their involvement in church completely turned around because we all prayed together. Jesus Himself promised that when two or three pray together (Matt. 18:20) and when two or more agree to pray for something (Matt. 18:19), it will be given to them. There is something powerful about praying together and uniting in purpose.

During this same time, God gave the church a new pastor who was a spiritual man, a man of prayer, energy, enthusiasm, and vision. When he preached, people *really* listened. The messages were spiritual and practical. The church was growing, and God was pouring His blessings.

I'm Going to Marry Her

While all this was going on, God gave me one of His greatest gifts in my life. I married the most beautiful woman in the world.

I'd first seen her when I was just six years old. She was only age three, walking into the church holding her sister's hand. I was approaching the church with my older sister and immediately stopped when I saw her.

"What's wrong?" my sister asked.

"Just look at that girl," I whispered. "She's amazing!"

"Who? Where?"

"There," I pointed while staring. "She's so pretty! I'm going to marry her!"

"You don't even know what love means, Lucu. You are going to change your mind a hundred times. You are going to forget that girl when you are older. You won't even think about her."

"Yes, I will marry her!" I shot back. "She's *different*! She's . . . she's . . . " I searched for the most extravagant compliment my six-year-old mind could think of—"She's beautiful!" I finished triumphantly. "She walks like a cat!"

Her name was Daniela, and I kept my eyes on her from then on. I learned everything I could about her. I knew she liked vanilla ice cream. I didn't like vanilla. I loved pistachio ice cream. But I made myself like vanilla too, to be like her. I knew the perfume she liked, the colors, the music, and everything else. I even got myself a lovely, expensive handkerchief, sprayed it with the perfume she liked most, and kept it for when she'd need one. If there was ever a tear that dropped, I was there—and ready.

Later, we both were in the church choir. I sang tenor; she sang alto. During sermons, everyone else looked at the pastor, but my head was turned toward her. It was like I had a spring turning my head in that direction. And, at times, I caught her looking at me, too.

We attended the same school, and I made sure that I regularly "happened" to walk to school at the same time she was going.

One day I finished school an hour earlier but waited outside of school to "casually" run into Daniela and say that I was out of school at the same time. But she surprised me by somehow just appearing next to me when a large group of students came out of school. "Why are you still here?" she asked. "I know you finished an hour ago. Are you waiting for me?"

"Uhh, yeah," I responded sheepishly.

"You know, I missed a class yesterday just so that we could go home together."

Hearing that, I was so excited! My heart felt like it was beating out of my chest. I had a *huge* grin on my face.

"That makes me happy. And I would like to date you, but I do not want to just have a casual relationship, just to date and then break up. I would like to date you with the intention of marrying you in the future."

She thought about that and then said, "I've always thought you're cute, but in the beginning, I didn't like that you won every competition. You are the center of every group you are in. Girls flock to you.

"Then I began to see that you are a good-hearted person and a very capable man. I started to like you. But there is one problem. My desire has always been to serve Jesus, so I would like to marry a pastor. And you plan to be an engineer. So we cannot date."

I started to smile. "Actually, I am only studying engineering at university to get a reduced term on army service. But God called me to be a pastor when I was a kid and, eventually, I will get there."

She smiled back and said, "Now I know that this is from God." We were both excited to know that this was going to work.

I memorized everything about her—her expression, her face, her eyes, her smile. I would go home, close my eyes, and see her in my mind. I would dream about her, think about her, write poetry, and sing songs for her.

I sometimes imagine how our love for Jesus would be if we did the same thing with Him—if our minds and eyes couldn't help but be fixed on Him.

Often my friends would say, "Stop staring at her all the time." But I always answered, "I love her. I am going to marry her." Our devotion for each other never wavered.

As our friendship grew, we studied and talked together about God. Our love for Him became stronger, and her prayers followed me through years of hard times. Her faith in God's promises strengthened my own.

During college, we got married. Our wedding day was beyond anything I'd dreamed. And as I write this today, I'm happy to say that God's blessings have carried us through thirty-six wonderful years of marriage thus far. Our love grows deeper and more profound every day.

Right after our wedding, we returned to Bucharest so I could continue school. Daniela started attending the church I was a member of. I couldn't wait to introduce her to our praying youth group and have her become part of our loving, growing church.

That first Sabbath as a married couple, I stood to sing the opening hymn beside my new wife—surrounded by this dedicated, Spirit-filled church that was now on fire for God.

I could never have imagined that a time was coming when Daniela and I would stand side-by-side with these dear members through a devastating trial. Or how seriously our faith would be tested.

The Devil Gets Angry

As I mentioned, we had a new pastor at the Bucharest church who was absolutely amazing. God sent us an extraordinarily devoted and capable young man. His sermons continued to revive and grow the church.

People heard about him and came to listen. The loving members welcomed them, and many more joined our fellowship.

Our entire church family became alive.

Within two years of when we first started praying, God developed and prepared us for what was to come. In the process of answering our prayers, God gave us time to know Him better and trust Him more. He knew we needed faith for what would happen next.

Every time God begins working in His church, Satan always sends conflicts. He attacks viciously. I've seen it so many times. I always remind myself, "This is war. It is the great controversy between God and Satan."

I remember one time when I began a series of evangelistic meetings that our septic tank at home overflowed into our basement. No one could figure out why.

Another time, I was driving to the airport in my nice Nissan Maxima, and the engine literally fell out of the car onto the interstate.

Once, right when I was ready to leave for Germany for an evangelistic meeting, a tree fell on my car during a sudden storm.

Satan hates what we do.

Recently, I was to speak to the seminary faculty and students at

Andrews University. On my way there, I was to first stop at 3ABN and tape an important program to be broadcast worldwide.

I was driving, praying for Jesus' presence and leading, asking that He would bless these talks and make them something special that He could use to His glory.

Suddenly, with no warning, a huge hole appeared in front of me on the interstate. I could not avoid it and hit it head-on. The front right wheel was completely destroyed. The back right wheel had significant damage, forming a bulging bubble that could explode anytime. But I only had one spare.

I pulled to the side of the road. It was half-past midnight, so all tire stores were closed. I spent over an hour moving my good rear wheel to the front right, then my spare and the less-damaged front wheel to the back.

Now I could drive, but only up to fifty miles per hour (mph). Otherwise, the whole car would shake, and the tire bubble would explode.

I kept praying, "Lord, I need the confidence to know You are with me. This is war; Satan is attacking me. I need your presence, and I can't drive on this type of wheel without You. I need confirmation that You will keep me safe, get me there on time, and bless my efforts to serve You. Should I stay here and forget it—or should I keep driving? What is Your will?"

As I prayed, I glanced at my fuel indicator. My car was only a year old and very accurate. I had 332 miles left to drive at my current fuel level, so I didn't have to stop for gas right away. But it would be impossible to get to 3ABN on time, going 50 mph, without a miracle.

So I bumped along, continuing to pray. "Lord, I need to know You are with me." Two hours later, the fuel gauge still said that I had 332 miles left to go. *That's strange,* I thought to myself. *I've driven two hours and still have the same amount of gas.*

I kept creeping along and praying. I prayed for safety, the speech at Andrews, the taping at 3ABN. I prayed for *Ministry* Magazine, for the whole team there. Mile after mile, hour after hour. The fuel gauge still read that I had 332 miles of gas left. I knew Jesus was telling me that He was with me. I realized that even though Satan was attacking, Jesus turned that attack into a miracle.

I drove through the night to reach 3ABN in time without ever having to stop for fuel. I got there only half an hour before I began speaking at 8:00 a.m. When I was finished taping, I replaced all four tires and the damaged rims. Only when I got on the road again did the numbers on my fuel gauge start slowly going down.

The Gates of Hell

When the Holy Spirit was poured out on our church in Bucharest, we experienced a revival and were growing. Satan became so angry and attacked hard. It was war.

I was still only a student. There were many church members, many elders, and many in leadership who knew even more details and were more involved in all that happened next. We learned that the president of Romania was rebuilding that section of the city. Our church, plus many other buildings, was in the way. One day, the police came and announced, "We are going to demolish this church."

How we all prayed! The church leadership tried to negotiate. They tried to appeal. Surely God would not allow this life-giving, active, vibrant, healthy church to be destroyed.

I remember the day we got word that bulldozers and a crane were approaching the property. Most members ran to the church immediately, including Daniela and me. Daniela was now pregnant with our first child, Gabriel.

We all joined together to form a chain of people around the walls of our beautiful church. We knew the government workers wouldn't go through human bodies with their wrecking equipment.

The police arrived and set up around the entire perimeter of the church. They didn't immediately arrest us because word spread even through neighboring countries about the government demolishing churches, including ours, so the press came to cover the story. And since other countries watched the coverage, the government didn't want to look bad.

The stand-off began. As long as we stood around the church, the demolition crews would not move forward. But the police also knew we couldn't stay there forever. They surrounded us—waiting for us to grow so hungry that we would give in.

The days passed. Those were hard, hard, long days. Day and night, we stood in front of that church. We took shifts between being a human fence around the church and going inside to sleep, eat, and pray together. We kept encouraging each other. Why would God allow our church to be destroyed? He had brought such revival! Surely He wouldn't let that be stopped by police, wrecking crews, or anything else.

Some of our people had to leave to go to work. The police would let them out but never back in again. I don't know how many days passed. But every day, more of our members needed to leave. The police knew they were starving us out.

A few of our members managed to bring food in. Pitzi and I talked privately about how we could also bring in some food. There was a market nearby if we could only get out and somehow get the food back in. Together, we hashed out a plan.

We smeared our clothes with some dirt to blend in with the construction workers that worked at a site next door. When they left, we blended in with them and left, too. Once we were out, we headed straight for the market and bought a bunch of watermelons. That was the easy part.

Heading back to the church, we knew there was no way to sneak the watermelons past the police. Instead, I walked right up to them and started a conversation.

"What are you doing here?" I asked.

"Oh, we surrounded that group of Seventh-day Adventists. Their church needs to be demolished. And what do they do? They don't leave. They are stubborn. They believe God is going to do something for them."

"Well, here," I said, "I have watermelons. Have some!"

While I was busy handing watermelons to the police, Pitzi slipped past them. I kept talking while discretely rolling watermelons, one by one, on the ground behind me with my foot toward Pitzi, who took them to the church members. We did that a few times.

Under the bridge area where we passed by, the officers noticed that we were not part of the workers that came to demolish the church. They quickly realized what we were trying to do. But they chose to turn a blind eye. One of them said, "Some of us don't want to demolish your church, but it's our job. We know that you try to bring some food to the people there, but as far as we are concerned, we don't care."

Over the next few days, Pitzi and I repeated our trips, bringing back bread, tomatoes, cucumbers, peppers, drinks, and cookies. Chocolate, too.

The tension over the stand-off ran so high, and the international press reported the story with so much unfavorable publicity that even President Ceausescu came to assess the situation from a distance.

He ordered that demolition should move ahead—no matter the cost.

Soon, the crane started to hit the building with its big, gigantic steel ball. The noise of the beams cracking and giant pieces of walls falling grew horrendous. The choir director, a wonderful man, asked the choir to sing one more song before the building toppled. We sang "My Jerusalem." People were crying and praying.

Dust and debris rained down around us. The police moved in, shouting and cursing, shoving us aside. But we stayed until there was no more building behind us. I'll never forget the huge pile of rubble. Just like that, our church was gone. Why would God allow this?

After all the revival of the past few years, after all these hard days standing against the demolition crew with the whole country—even much of the world—watching, why did God permit this destruction?

The pastor told us,
"If God allowed this, He has a plan.
We need to keep praying."

And, right then, our whole church declared war on Satan. We said, "We're going to keep praying. We are going to ask God to give us more churches instead of just this one!"

For the next months, many people prayed. Some in the morning, some later in the day. The Holy Spirit began to move even more than before. Do you know what happened? First, the church members found land, put up a tent, and kept meeting every Sabbath. Our congregation began to grow. We overflowed so much that we split into two congregations.

And the address where first we put up a tent, and then later built a nice church—777 Victorious Street! The church kept praying and growing. Another church was built. And another. God multiplied four new churches out of one demolished church.

". . . I will build My church;
and the gates of hell shall not prevail against it."
Matthew 16:18 (KJV)

God loves a praying church!

SUMMARY

Everything we do must begin with prayer and be immersed in prayer. Pray and work, work and pray.

Too often, we struggle in prayer because we want instant answers. But answers to prayer are a process. As we keep praying, God keeps working.

Many times, God allows us to pray more so that we learn to care more about what we pray for.

The more we pray, the more we learn how to pray. Spiritual growth is not an event. We don't grow spiritually in just one day. We grow every day as long as we live.

4 CHAPTER

SEE YOU NEXT THURSDAY

Many years later, Daniela and I, with our two sons, moved to the United States. After graduating from seminary at Andrews University, I became a pastor of a multichurch district. One of my churches had a member named Martha. Every church needs a member like her.

Martha worked harder than anybody I've seen in my life. She had great ideas, and she knew how to get them done. You could not have a more dedicated person on your team. She also shared a trait with me—she talked a *lot*. She even talked *more* than I do. I mean, she could talk until the Second Coming, and she would not get tired.

My church was small yet filled with wonderful people. My English was just terrible, and they struggled to understand my words. But everyone was so protective and caring of me. Often on Sabbath, Martha and her husband, Robert, invited us to their home for Sabbath dinner, and we would have great conversations.

Robert didn't talk as much as his wife, but he often quoted Jeremiah 33:3.

***"Call to me and I will answer you,
and I will tell you great and mighty things,
which you do not know" (NASB).***

This promise grew to be life-changing for our little congregation.

Our town was small, and we tried to do evangelism. But nobody came to our creaky little church. Times were hard, and people were more concerned with paying their bills and putting food on the table than hearing about prophecy.

We had no baptisms.

So, I preached about prayer to our members. I told them we needed to pray because that was how we connected to our Source of power. I told them that the more we prayed, the more we would hear God's voice and know His plan for our church.

We needed God's plan if we were to have His blessing and power and do anything successfully. I reminded them that it is not by our power but by God's Spirit (Zech. 4:6), and the Holy Spirit and revival come as a result of dedicated prayer.

Martha came to me after the sermon and said, "I want God's vision for our church. How do I hear God's voice? How do I listen when I pray?"

"Well," I answered, "you pray a little, then be silent for a few seconds. He may speak, or He may not, but be silent. Wait quietly and give Him a chance—but don't tell Him when to talk. You just wait. Pray and think and study. Prayer and study of the Word always go together; they cannot be separated. Through prayer, you talk to God, and He talks to you through His Word. Prayer should be a conversation. Digest what you study and reflect on it. Pray over what you read, asking God for wisdom and His Holy Spirit. God promised wisdom and His Spirit to those who ask." She nodded and listened.

"Then you pray again," I continued. "Then you read a little and think about it. Keep praying, reading, thinking; praying, reading, thinking."

Prayer is a dialogue, not a monologue.

"Sometimes," I went on, "I will read the same verse repeatedly fifteen—twenty times— because that stores it in my heart. Then the Holy Spirit will give it to me later when I need it most."

"Finally, make yourself available to do what God asks of you. When God calls, you will know."

"Okay," Martha said, "I will pray that way."

A few weeks later, she called me. "Pastor, God talked to me! But why did it take Him so long?"

"Because He had to prepare you," I told her. "If He had answered you in the beginning, you would not have been ready. He had to prepare you for what He has in store for you."

How Do We Really Know God's Voice?

Is there a way to be sure that God is really speaking to us? What if it's just our own thoughts?

First, I've found that if I pray just duty prayer—if I don't pray and spend time in His Word, I may *not* know the difference. But spending time in dedicated prayer and studying the Word makes us sensitive to God's leading. The more we pray and study, the more we know Him and how He works. The more we study and discover how He's worked in the past, the more we can see God's leading today because He is consistent. God doesn't change.

You cannot know someone's voice unless you spend time with that person. Unless you talk with them again and again. I will not recognize your voice if you call me if we never talk. But if my wife, Daniela, calls me, she doesn't need to introduce herself. I know her voice. And, most of the time, I even know what she wants to say. We talk about everything. We have spent so much time together that we know what the other is thinking just by seeing each other's faces.

If I travel, I don't go to sleep before we talk and check up on each other. For instance, I must often eat as I have a fast metabolism. She knows that and calls me to remind me to eat a little. She says, "Honey, how are you? Did you manage to eat an apple or a banana or a sandwich?"

"I will do it in a minute," I reply.

"I will call you back to make sure you do it. I love you," she says.

Then she calls back. "Did you manage to put something in your stomach?"

"I did."

"Good, I love you." When I'm driving home and go between mountains, I sometimes lose cell reception. If she calls, all I hear is, "How are . . . chhhhhhh . . . make sure that you . . . chhhhhh . . . apple . . . chhhhhh . . . love . . . chhhhhhhh . . . ."

How do I know that is her even with the bad connection? I know her voice and her message. She is always consistent.

How do you know God's voice? Keep talking to Him about everything. The more you talk and listen through prayer and study of the Word, the more you know Him. And the more you understand His message and voice.

Also, our own thoughts tend to follow what we like—things that make us comfortable. And we are inclined to do things that are logical to us. God's plans and thoughts are far from our plans and thoughts. He sees the whole picture—the beginning to the end. His plans usually don't make much sense to us humans. And most of the time they are big. They seem impossible. They feel very uncomfortable. We can't understand Him because we don't have His brain. We just need to trust Him.

God sent Abraham to a far country. He sent Moses to Pharaoh. And He sent Elijah to Ahab. None of these trips were either comfortable or logical.

God asked Joshua to walk around Jericho and Gideon to go to war with only 300 people and no weapons. That was not logical at all.

God asked Naaman to bathe seven times in Jordan to cure him of his leprosy. This made no sense. He asked Noah to build an ark. What was an ark, anyway, and why build one?

I'm Listening, But . . .

I once gave a seminar at one of our academies where I talked about listening when we pray. Afterward, the pastor talked with his wife and said, "Honey, I want to do this. From now on, I want us to listen every day to God. I want us to make ourselves available for God's plan and service." She agreed.

A week or so later, he called me. "Pavel, I'm listening, but God doesn't talk to me."

I said, "Hey, Buddy! We cannot tell Him when to talk and when to keep quiet. We just need to keep praying, studying, and be open to His leading. We need to walk with Him, remain in Him, and stay connected. *He* decides when to talk and when not to talk. Just make yourself available. He knows when He has a job for you. And He will find a way to let you know if you are open and connected."

A few more weeks went by, and my telephone rang again.

"Pavel, you won't believe what happened."

"Try me," I said because I know how God works.

He said, "Every day, I pray and study and think, and I make myself available for His plan. I pray and say, 'Lord, please, if You have something for me today, make it clear, give me the opportunity, help me to see it and hear it, and I will do Your will.'

"Yesterday, I prayed the same prayer again, and, as usual, God was silent. But my wife and I left the house to do some errands. As I was driving along, I heard a voice in my brain saying, 'Go to the academy.'

"I told my wife, 'Honey, I think God impressed me to go to the academy.'

"She said, 'It's school vacation—nobody's there. It must be your own mind.'

"I said, 'Honey, it's not my mind. If it were my mind, it would have said, "Go to Olive Garden!" It's God's voice. And it doesn't make sense. Why would I want to go to school during vacation?'

" 'So,' she said, 'Okay! Let's go!'

"I turned the van around and drove to the academy. As we pulled up to the front gate, I saw a guy standing there. When we got closer, I could see he was crying.

" 'What are you doing here?' I asked him.

"He said, 'Twenty-one years ago, I was a student in this school. They caught me on drugs, and I got expelled. I continued using drugs and eventually became a dealer. I got caught and went to prison. When I finally got out, I didn't want to ever go back. I knew I needed Christ. But I didn't know how to change. I needed help. So I came here because this is where I learned about Jesus and His love. But the doors were locked. I've been standing here praying, 'Lord, send somebody that can help me.' "

Does God still talk to His people?

Yes! God did it in the Bible, and He is still doing it now. He never changes.

God Told Me to Look

I shared this message with a group in Michigan. A man there named James heard the story and began praying this same prayer.

He told his wife, "Honey, we need to keep praying and listening for God's voice instead of listening to the news on the radio when we drive. We need to be available for God's plan today, tomorrow, every day." So they turned off the radio and prayed every day.

After a few weeks, they were driving through snow one afternoon. God impressed him to look to the right. He turned his head and saw something. "Honey, I saw something like a white bump in the snow."

She said, "Snow *is* white."

"No, no, no. God impressed me to look there."

"Honey, it is your mind."

"NO, it is not just my mind. It was God's voice."

He got off the next exit, turned around, went back to the previous exit, and re-entered the highway, driving slowly and watching on the right. Far out in the field, he saw what looked like a little white bump in the snow. He parked the car on the shoulder and walked over.

Sure enough, there was an older gentleman with gray hair wearing a thin white robe. He had a band around his wrist with his name and the word "Alzheimer." The man had wandered outside the nursing home and gotten confused and lost. Now he was snowed over and nearly frozen.

James took the elderly man in his arms and got him into his SUV. He took him to the nearest hospital. The doctor told James that he'd found the gentleman at the last moment—it had almost been too late.

Later that day, the gentleman's daughter called James. "The doctor told me what happened. Thank you for saving my father. I'm so glad you didn't hit him with your car!"

"I couldn't have hit him. He was nowhere near the road—just out in the middle of a field."

"If he wasn't on the interstate, how did you see him?"

"You wouldn't believe me if I told you."

"Tell me."

"God talked to me and told me to look to the right."

"What? God talked to you?"

"Yes. The Bible says that 'My sheep know me and hear my voice.' That's what happened."

"That can't be. God talked to people in the past but not today."

"Yes, He still talks to us. We just don't listen."

"I'd like to join your church."

"Why?"

"Because the churches I go to just talk theory, but your church has a real God who talks to you now."

God knows the plans He has for us—the problem is that *we* don't know. We pray, "May Your will be done!" But to do His will, we need to first know it. And to know His will, we need to listen, to make ourselves available. Then we need to obey.

We'll Never Reach Our Town That Way

"I know what God wants me to do," Martha now told me. "He impressed me that we will never reach the people in our town by doing evangelism and Bible studies alone. We need to feed them—they are hungry. We need to help them. We need to build relationships. Then we can lead them to Jesus. We need to have a community center."

"What does that imply?" I asked, feeling a bit wary.

"Well, we need a building. We need food, furniture, and clothing. We need anything that people need. Anything that they use. If they don't have a table, we give them a table. And then we pray with them when they come to pick up the food. We need to build friendships." She was talking about Christ's method. First, He mingled with people and cared for their needs. Then He said, "Follow Me."

"Well, good for you, Martha!" I said, smiling my best pastor smile. "God bless you, sister. Go and do it."

"Pastor," she said, "*you* told me to pray this way. Now *you* need to help me start it!"

In my mind, I thought, *Yeah, yeah, yeah. God gave you the vision. Why didn't He give it to me? I'm the pastor.* However, God gave her the idea because she prayed a lot about it, and I didn't.

"Okay, what do you want me to do?" I asked.

Martha already had a list. "We need a location," she said. "Meet me here, and we'll go together to find one."

"Okay. Thursday morning at 9:00. I will give you half an hour."

She said, "Pastor—half an hour? We can hardly go to one place with that time. We need to go from door to door, business to business, to find a building to rent!"

"Then I will do 9:00 a.m. to noon," I said. "My afternoon is busy."

"Okay, three hours," she agreed.

See You Next Thursday

On Thursday morning, I rode into the church parking lot and parked. Promptly at 9:00 a.m., Martha pulled her van alongside me. Off we went together, knocking on doors.

We found nothing. Either the place was too small, too junky, leaking, or way too expensive. Of course, Martha had already done the math. "We can't rent anything above $2,500 a month," she told me.

The cheapest we found was $4,000 per month—nearly double. At the end of our three-hour hunt, I said, "Okay, Martha, we tried. I guess we'll pray some more and see what happens next. God bless you."

"OK, Pastor," she beamed, "I'll see you next Thursday!"

"No, no, no. I didn't say 'Thursdays' plural," I protested, "I said Thursday—singular."

"Pastor, you taught in the prayer seminar that we need to be persistent. You said that if we want God to give us a blessing, we need not try one time and then give up. We need to be dedicated and diligent. You said that we need to mean it with all our heart."

Martha had listened to my sermons better than I had. And she was right.

So the following Thursday, we went again. And the next Thursday. We knocked on any promising door. We visited every suitable business. Eventually, we finished the town.

"Well, Martha," I said, "It looks like we don't have anywhere else to go. We tried everywhere."

"See you next Thursday, Pastor!" she replied.

"What? Why?"

"We'll go over to the next town. Maybe God wants us to reach that town."

Thursday after Thursday after Thursday. Every door was knocked on.

We finished the second town. "See you next Thursday!"

"Why? Is there another town next to this?"

"No, we'll start back again in the first one."

"We did that already!" My head was beginning to spin.

"Maybe something just opened!" she said.

"Are you *sure* God told you this?"

"Pastor, I ask myself every night why God hasn't given us a location yet and why it's taking so long. He keeps impressing me to be persistent, keep knocking, and not doubt. I remember that you said we don't need to understand to obey. You said we could not understand why God says to build an ark or walk around Jericho. And if we try to understand, we will never obey. You said we just need to trust Him and keep going. In your sermon, you even sang a few words from the song, 'Trust and Obey.' You said that answer to prayer usually is not an event but a process. That God has to prepare us for His plan and prepare the others, and the place. And we need to keep praying and working. Remember what you said, 'Those who wait upon the Lord.' So, we need to wait for God's timing. See you next Thursday, Pastor."

She was preaching my sermon back at me! I began to feel bad that I actually hadn't prayed enough. So *my* prayers began to change, and I kept going with her. Back to the first town. Finished it again. Back to the second town. Starting over.

Every Thursday morning. Month after month. I got so tired of going from door to door every Thursday morning that I was ready to move from the district.

But Martha never lost her faith. She never got tired. She never lost her commitment. She kept smiling and kept searching. "Let's keep going!" she'd say every time.

"How long?" I finally asked.

"Pastor, you said to pray and go *until* you have an answer!"

Oh, I was tired. I thought, *Lord, you really need to answer this prayer–either yes or no. But we need to put a limit to this.*

On we went. One Thursday, we returned to a business we'd visited several months earlier. It was a great location, but the owner wanted $4,500 per month. "Not a penny less," he said the first time.

Now he recognized us right away. "You've been here before," he greeted us.

"Yes."

"And you said the most you can pay is $2,500."

"Yes."

"I want $4,500."

"We don't have that," I said.

"What do you want it for?" he asked. "What business do you have?"

Martha spoke up, her enthusiasm undiminished. "Oh, we don't plan to open a business. We want to open a community center to help the community."

"Wow!" he said. "You're doing good work. You know what? The economy has dropped, and I can't rent this space out. I guess it's better for me to have $2,500 than nothing. You can have it for your amount."

Praise the Lord! I thought. *Next Thursday, I don't have to go again!*

"Let's sign the papers!" I said.

How Did You Know?

As we finished signing the contract, my cell phone rang. Not thirty minutes later, not five minutes later. Not a day later. Right as I finished signing, it rang.

I answered even though I didn't recognize the number.

"Hello, are you Pastor Goia?" the caller asked.

"Yes."

"I'm the General Manager of K-Mart. We're closing the store, and I wondered if you would like our shelving for your community center?"

I was shocked. "How did you know we were starting a community center?" I asked.

He said, "*Everybody* knows you're starting a community center—you've been knocking on doors for months."

The whole town now knew that a little Seventh-day Adventist church was starting a community center to help people. I began to understand that God allowed us to keep knocking on the doors until the community learned about us and our plans.

Our head elder took his truck down and picked up the shelving from K-mart. We couldn't fit it all in the center, so we put the extra shelves out in the parking area. Clothes and donations began to pour in. Churches from other denominations began calling, wanting to be involved, and heading up drives among their members for clothes and furniture.

When Hurricane Katrina hit, our little community center began sending down 18-wheeler trucks filled with clothes. And still, the donations poured in.

I marveled how our little church would have been far too small to support all that was happening. I could see that God wanted us to knock on every door so that the whole town would learn about this incredible project and become a part of it.

We started a prayer group at the community center on Tuesday nights. We would pray for everyone who came and give them a book like *Steps to Christ*. We began to build friendships, and people said, "This church is great. They help us; they pray for us. They are the church that represents Jesus in our community. They care!"

By now, many more of our wonderful members were involved. They added their prayers, skills, and donations to Martha's community center, and our operation kept growing.

The phone rang again. The local government called to ask if we could handle the distribution of food stamps. We said yes. Then they called and asked if we could help some of the people out of jail on probation by mentoring and training them as volunteers and teaching them skills while they transitioned? We said yes.

The whole town now called it "*our* community center." Not "your community center." We were a town project. We were making a difference. The local newspaper interviewed us and put us on the cover page.

Meanwhile, our church started to have visitors. We had some Bible studies. We also had evangelism.

Praise the Lord! I thought.

"Praise the Lord!" all the busy church members said over and over.

And Guess What?

One day, here came Martha again. "Pastor, we should pray that God will expand our territory!"

"What do you mean?"

"We have no more room! We get so many donations that we can't fit them inside, so we put them outside on the shelves in the parking lot. Soon the rain and snow will come. We need to pray."

Once again, our community center group began praying. As we knelt together one morning, we heard a knock on the door. It was the owner of the business next door.

"I must close half of my business in the winter because my utilities cost so much," he told us. "I see your things outside there, and bad weather will be here soon. You can move all these shelves and clothes into the rear part of my building as long as you don't turn on the heat."

Martha asked, "How much do we owe you for that?"

He answered, "You can have it for free. You're helping the community, and I want to be part of your blessings."

Praise the Lord! We moved the overflow into the rear of his building. But soon, we filled that space, and donations kept coming. We kept praying.

Three months later, in the middle of winter, our business neighbor on the other side stopped by. "You know," he told us, "that guy who let you use the back of his building told me that in three months, God blessed him with more sales in his reduced space than when he had his whole business open. I want to give you half of my building, too. Maybe God will bless me as well."

Within a year, we grew so big that we had to purchase a bigger building. And the whole town knew about our church and community center.

Why? Because one lady was ready to *really* pray. Because one lady was willing to *listen* and *wait* for God's timing. And because she was then ready to work with enthusiasm and commitment. And because the whole church became so involved when God answered.

All during those long months, looking at buildings every Thursday morning, praying and not receiving answers—all that time, God was actually working, preparing us and the town for His plan. He wanted everyone to learn about it and be involved.

We didn't have to convince the church visitors about anything—they saw God in our love and our behavior. They saw Christ's character reproduced in His children.

All because of persistent prayer. All in God's plan. And through His power.

SUMMARY

Prayer is a dialogue, not a monologue.

Pray, study, think it over, pray again. Make it a conversation. Listen for God. Make yourself available to Him. He knows when He has a job for you and He will find a way to let you know if you listen and if you are open to His plan.

Answer to prayer is a process. God sometimes takes a while to work with us and prepare us for what He is going to do.

When God talks, He doesn't talk small—because God is not small. God talks big. He talks so big that we cannot wrap our minds around what He says.

But when we start praying, God starts working. Even though we cannot understand His plans, He needs us to know Him so well that we are not trying to understand in order to obey. Rather, we trust Him so much that we will obey anything He asks us to do.

CHAPTER 5

WHAT WILL HE DO? DISFELLOWSHIP US?

I love the mountains. If you put me in a small cabin in the mountains by a stream of water or lake, I would be happy. All I need is two books, flowing water, and mountains. And food—lots of food.

My friend, Pitzi, and I basically climbed every mountain in Romania through the years. Sometimes on our own and sometimes with our church group. When we were teenagers, our pastor, Brother Traian (Try-an), would take the youth camping in the mountains several times a year.

Brother Traian was energetic, courageous, humble, and ready to sacrifice. He didn't usually get too bothered when Pitzi and I played jokes. He'd say, "You boys are the first to pull pranks, but you are also the first to attend Bible studies, programs, and youth meetings."

Brother Traian and his wife, Sister Irina, didn't have kids of their own. They were very warm and kind to us. They would invite us to eat with them often despite our pranks. "You're our boys," they'd say.

They lived right beside the church. The church building was L-shaped. If you went in the church's front door and turned right, the committee room and a stairway were there. If you went up the stairs, you could either go into the church balcony or turn right and go into the attic over the pastor's house.

Soon after they moved in, I said to Pitzi, "I have an idea. Let's go in the attic." We sneaked up the church stairs and tiptoed across the attic to where a stainless-steel funnel over their kitchen stove opened up. We called it a *hota*—a hood. It didn't have a filter or exhaust fan. It was primitive. Literally, just a hole that let the steam into the attic.

We could hear Brother Traian and Sister Irina talking in the kitchen below. We knew they loved each other, but they were having a polite argument on this night.

"Honey, I'm so hungry," Brother Traian said. "Aren't you finished cooking yet? Is supper almost ready?"

"Not yet. But you can help, and it will go faster."

"I can't. I have to finish my sermon."

"Then be patient. I'm working on it."

Pitzi and I grinned at each other as an idea formed. We knew how important food was to Brother Traian.

We enjoyed the aroma floating up to us from the pot of soup as we waited for our opportunity. When Sister Irina left the kitchen for a few minutes, I whispered to Pitzi, "Let's do it!"

We had brought a long wire that I bent at the end to make a hook. I then let it down through the *hota*, using the hook to lift the lid on the pot of soup. I poured two or three cups of salt into the soup and then put the lid back.

We could hardly keep quiet a few minutes later when Brother Traian sat down at the table and took his first spoonful of soup. He spat it right back out.

"Irina! This soup is terrible!"

Now she was upset. "If you don't like it, then you cook!"

"Honey," he said, "you are usually a good cook. But what happened? You put in so much salt!"

"Honey, I put normal salt as always," she answered.

"No. You must taste it."

"I already did. When I made it."

"Here. Take a spoonful."

A pause, and then we heard her make a little choking sound. "Oh, you are right! It's terrible! I don't know what happened!"

Brother Traian said, "Ah, well. Don't worry. We'll just forget it. Let's make potatoes or something."

"Ok," she said.

Pitzi and I snuck out silently, snickering all the way. The next day we told each other, "Let's do it again!"

But when we got there that afternoon, we found something even better to do. We could see their washing hanging on wires all around the terra cotta stove in the kitchen because they didn't have a clothes dryer.

Brother Traian and Sister Irina were gone when we arrived, so we quickly took each piece of laundry and hung them all over the large apple tree beside the church. The tree was in the front yard facing the street, making it even funnier.

Then we hid in the attic again to hear their reactions when they came home. We didn't have long to wait.

"Honey!" Sister Irina's voice was raised. "I asked you to hang the clothing to dry. But *why* would you hang them outside? They all got dirty. Now I have to wash them again."

"No, honey. I didn't put them outside," Brother Traian said, sounding confused.

"Well, you have lost your mind," she retorted, "because they are all hanging in the apple tree."

Just at that moment, I moved by mistake, making a scraping noise. They both realized immediately what was going on.

"Aha!" Sister Irina almost shouted—and she was really boiling. "It's not *you* with the salt—it's Pitzi and Lucu! It's not *you* with the clothes—it's Pitzi and Lucu! You kids ruined my soup!"

Brother Traian was trying not to laugh. "Now, Irina, leave them alone. They are our kids. We love them."

"Kids need boundaries," she snapped back. "Don't you see all the stuff they do?"

"That's ok," he said, "That means they are smart." To us, he said, "You boys have lots of ideas. And you are always the most energetic. But you must be sure to use your ideas in a good way, or you will do something you regret later."

Sister Irina was too sweet to stay upset for long.

I Told You to Put Boundaries

One time the pastor and his wife took the church youth group camping near the Black Sea. On this particular trip, we pitched our tents on the beach beside a lake called Techirghiol, which is so salty that you cannot sink. I mean, you can sit in the water and read the newspaper. When the wind blows, it literally makes stripes of salt on the water.

The first night, when I saw how soundly Brother Traian slept, I got an idea. But I shared my idea with Sister Irina first—and she allowed me to go ahead.

"Hey everyone," I said, "why don't we have fun with the pastor?"

Many of them were shocked. "Oh no! We can't do that!"

"What will he do?" I asked. "Disfellowship us?"

I finally persuaded everyone.

We took Brother Traian, sound asleep on his inflatable air mattress, and put him on the lake. Then we pushed him slowly out a little way from the shore.

After we gathered silently back on the beach, I gave the signal.

All together, we shouted, "BROTHER TRAIAN! THE PHILISTINES ARE UPON YOU!"

I've never seen anyone move so fast. He sat straight up, lost his balance, and fell into the lake.

Everyone laughed so hard we could barely stand. "Pitzi and Lucu!" he roared, "I know this was you! I'm going to tell your fathers."

Now Sister Irina laughed even more. "Aha! I told you to put boundaries!" she called to him. He huffed around a few more minutes but never stayed upset very long either.

Instead, he showed me what a true pastor looked like.

Brother Traian didn't just preach about God. He and Sister Irina were filled with the Holy Spirit and lived God's grace by how they treated us.

They were so patient with Pitzi and me—so quick to invite us to their home. So willing to laugh and forgive our jokes. Always encouraging us.

"We know that God has a plan for you guys," Brother Traian would say. "He will accomplish so much through both of you."

Why Short Prayers Are Needed

Someone once asked me, "Did your pastor and his wife ever see how God eventually led you into ministry? Did they know what God did through you and Pitzi when you grew up?"

As I write this book, Brother Traian and Sister Irina are both enjoying retirement. Just a couple of years ago, when I was back in Romania to preach, Pitzi and I drove together to where they were living. It was so wonderful to see them again! Even though we couldn't stay long, we quickly enjoyed reliving some of the best memories, including the youth camping trips to the mountains or the sea.

We went to Caraiman, to Herculane, and so many other places. At Caraiman, we went through a dangerous place where the path became very narrow called The Horn. In a few places, there was no path but only a cable to hang from for a short way until there was a place to put your feet again. Pitzi and I, instead of going safely on the path like everyone else, decided to slide on the snow between the very close walls. The snow slope was narrow and going almost vertically straight down. I remember Sister Irina screaming, "You will die! Go like everyone else on the path!"

One of my most vivid memories came when they took our youth group to a mountain peak near a lovely tourist spot. I was about seventeen years old. As usual, all of the normal people (which was everyone except Pitzi and me) hiked up the regular path. It wound up one side of the mountain with a nice, slanted incline. There were several comfortable places to take a break and eat.

But Pitzi and I decided to climb up the hard way. The other side of the mountain went straight up from the valley floor, nearly vertical in many places, with only narrow ledges here and there. We didn't have any climbing equipment, not even a rope. We just went up.

When you go bare-hand rock climbing, it's extremely dangerous. Believe me! Once you get high enough, there is no way to go back.

On that day, we kept going, and going, and going. We got to the point where we were exhausted and shaking. We reached a narrow ledge and paused to rest a moment. Even then, we didn't let go of our handholds and were breathing hard. Pitzi said, "Don't look down."

"Why?" I asked, starting to look. I immediately stopped. The valley floor was far below us—with nothing but air in between.

"We need to get up to the top," Pitzi said. "We will not be able to hold on for too much longer." He began climbing again. I went, too, just a little behind him.

We were almost to the top. The rest of our group were already there, and some of them were looking over the edge, watching us finish the climb.

I put my hands on the rock above me to take the next step. But I couldn't see a huge crack just over the ledge. As I started to pull my weight up, the rock broke away from the mountain. I lost my balance and tried to grab hold again. But I was already falling.

There was nothing I could do at that moment. I instantly knew I was falling to my death, followed by an abrupt jerk. Instead of continuing to fall, I was hanging upside down, staring at the valley below.

By God's grace, Pitzi and I were both wearing boots with heavy hooks to hold the shoelaces.

A hook from my boot caught on a hook of Pitzi's boot. Now I was swinging, head down, in the air—held by just a boot hook.

Do you know what I did next? I prayed like never before.

I *really* prayed. It was a short prayer. It's good to learn to pray short prayers now because you may need them in the future.

I said, "Lord, there is nothing I can do unless You help!"

Friends, sometimes we think that we have control. But we just pretend. We are not in control.

We like to believe that
we are in charge of our lives,
of our situations,
but we are not.

There is nothing that we can control—it is all in God's hands. We just do not like to acknowledge this because we are proud. But when your life is hanging by a boot hook, you are not proud anymore.

Some in the church group above us were screaming and crying. I remember hearing Sister Irina's voice, "O Lord, protect them! Pitzi and Lucu! Lord, protect them!"

I lifted my head from staring down and looked up at Pitzi. He'd gotten a firm grip on a rock with one hand and was reaching out with his other hand to grab a branch. I could sense the boot hook start bending—I could sense I was going.

Pitzi broke off the branch and held it down to me. I caught it with one hand, and, in that second, the hook slipped away, and my body reversed position—my legs went down, and I was now hanging onto that branch. I grabbed it with my other hand, too. Now my body was really swinging.

Pitzi said, “Don’t move. Hold still.”

I said, “It’s the wind. I’m not moving!” I was not even trying to breathe because I was afraid it would slip.

Pitzi used the momentum to move me slowly back and forth while I quickly looked for a handhold. “Move me to the right,” I said, and he did. He was shaking.

I kept one hand on the branch and reached out my right hand to grab the rock. And then my left hand. And I let the branch go.

I was so shaken. “Thank you, Lord,” I whispered.

Can You Imagine?

Even forty years later, sitting in the living room with Brother Traian and Sister Irina and Pitzi, I still remembered how I felt with my life hanging on a boot hook.

Our conversation went on, but soon it was time to leave. I remember Brother Traian looking at Pitzi and me for a long moment before speaking. I’ll always remember his words.

“Look at what God has accomplished through both of you,” he said. “Just look at how He’s using you. You both serve Him, each one in different ways. You take care of people. You preach the gospel. I am so privileged that I was your pastor!”

Can you imagine what our church would be like today if every church leader treated our youth like Brother Traian and Sister Irina? Can you picture what our church would be like today if every one of us showed our love for God by how we treated each other?

Instead, we proudly call ourselves Christians and eat our tofu and broccoli. But we're too self-centered to be gracious. Too proud to be forgiving. Too busy to encourage. Too selfish to show compassion to others who are different or annoying. Often it is easier for us to say a few words of rebuke instead of words of reassurance and hope.

Someone can have all the right doctrines and still have no clue how to show love.

When we don't understand how much we need grace,
then we don't receive grace.
And when we don't receive grace, we can't extend grace.
We can't give to others what we don't have ourselves.

So many in the church today do not have the oil of the Holy Spirit. They don't even know how to receive love, let alone share love. They *talk* a lot about Jesus and His sacrifice, yet Jesus doesn't seem to be very active in their lives. Instead, many are asleep, fooled by the thought that they're fine because they go to church, keep the doctrines, and know the Sabbath.

They don't realize they are not filled with the Holy Spirit. That they are destitute of oil. That they have no relationship with their Savior.

They think they are saved. But salvation isn't an event—it's a Person. Salvation is Jesus Christ living in us through His Spirit. That's why we sing "Into My Heart." When He lives in us through His Spirit, there will be transformation; there will be fruit—the fruit of the Spirit. There will be love and grace.

To seek the presence of the Holy Spirit, to seek renewal, to constantly be filled with the Holy Spirit is to be our first work. "By the power of the Holy Spirit the moral image of God is to be perfected in the character. We are to be wholly transformed into the likeness of Christ."[1]

When we have the Holy Spirit, we have oil. When we have oil, we have fire, light, and love. If we don't have the fire, we don't have the Spirit. If we don't have the light, we don't have the Spirit. If we don't have the power, we don't have the Spirit. And if we don't have love, we don't have the Spirit.

People don't keep coming to church because we have good programs. People keep coming back when they see God's presence and love.

SUMMARY

We need to pray for our Father in heaven to pour the Holy Spirit's anointing power over us and touch our hearts with His unbelievable, incredible, infinite, amazing grace. Only He can change us. We certainly cannot change ourselves.

We are changed by beholding. We need to focus our eyes on Christ, our salvation. The more we reflect, behold, and understand what He has done, the more we have passion and love for Him and for each other.

When people get together to pray for the Holy Spirit, we are transformed, our families are saved, our churches grow.

[1] Ellen G. White, *Ye Shall Receive Power*, 25.

CHAPTER 6

"KUM BA YAH"

When Pitzi and I were at the university in Bucharest, we also started taking church youth groups on camping trips to the mountains. I remember one trip because I got a phone call a few days before we went.

"Pavel," they said, "we are calling about our daughter. Do you remember Elena?"

"Of course, I remember. How is she?" I asked. We'd known each other as kids, but it had been years since I'd seen her.

"She's not doing well," they told me. "Could you please pray for her? She wants nothing to do with God. Nothing to do with church. She drinks a lot. And smokes. She said that if we even talk about God to her, she will change her phone number and never speak to us again."

"I will pray for Elena," I told them. "And I will have our youth group pray for her, too."

"Oh, thank you, Pavel. But remember, if you ever see her, do not talk about God or church. Do not try to act all friendly because she will hate you right away. Just talk about mountains and climbing. She loves that."

Work According to Your Prayers

I called my friends from the youth prayer group and added Elena's name to our list. Over a two-year period, several people we prayed for came back to church, and some were even baptized.

Now we prayed for wisdom and creativity on how to connect with Elena.

"We cannot invite her to church," I told everyone. "She will refuse. But let's invite her to go camping in the mountains with us." We wanted to use Christ's method and build a friendship with her.

Christ built friendships first.
Then He said, "Follow Me."

A few days later, I decided to call her. First, I prayed for wisdom and God's Spirit to lead the conversation. Then I called. When she answered, her voice was not friendly.

"Hello."

"Hello, Elena."

"Who is there?"

I couldn't say, *"I am Lucu,"* because she would say, *"Ah. From church. What do you want?"*

And I couldn't say, *"I am a friend,"* because she would say, *"Oh, I have no friends."*

So, I said, "I am your enemy."

"What?"

"You heard me."

"What do you want?"

"I want to make your life miserable."

"WHAT? You don't even know me," she replied.

"Well, I know you like mountains," I said. "And I can beat you at any contest with mountains." I knew she was very competitive.

Now she was intrigued. "How can you beat me?" she challenged. "I have been rock climbing *everywhere*—and also skiing."

"Not enough," I answered. "*I* have been to every mountain, every path, and every cabin in Romania. Literally. I have pictures from everywhere."

"Well," she continued, "*I* climbed this mountain, and that mountain—without a rope!"

I said, "That is children's play. I have climbed way more dangerous places without a rope." I told her briefly of my experiences at Herculane and Caraiman's Peak and other places. Then I mentioned the place where I almost died. I was hanging upside down, caught on a boot hook.

"Impossible! I've been there. People don't climb there. They die."

"My friend and I climbed with our bare hands. And I fell from there."

"If you fell from there, you would be dead."

"Well, I am alive. I dangled upside down from my boot hook."

She said, "What is *wrong* with you? You don't have a brain! And why did you call? Who are you?"

"You know me by now, Elena. I am Lucu. We grew up together. I called because I know that you like mountains. In two weeks, I am taking our youth group to one of the best mountains in Romania—most people don't even know it exists. And I don't want you to miss it."

"What mountain?" she asked.

"Borsa" (*Bor-scha*), I answered, "in Bucovina. It's wild, beautiful nature out there—with old monasteries. And there is a lake at the top of the mountain. And sparkling water comes out of the ground. The view is breathtaking. We will go there for a week. Are you coming?"

And she said, "I am *so* tempted to come."

"Why don't you?"

"Because you are the *church* youth. You are going to pray. You are going to get in a circle and sing 'Kum ba yah,' and I *hate* that. And you are going to call me to pray with you."

I said, "Listen. We don't *want* you to come to our prayer group."

"What?"

"We don't want you to join our study. Or prayer. Or singing."

"What?"

"Stop saying 'what' all the time," I teased her.

"Well, you are *supposed* to invite me to your prayer group. You are *supposed* to convert me."

I said, "No. We don't want you to study or sing with us."

"Why?"

"Finally, you don't say 'what.' You say 'why.' "

And she started to laugh. The ice was broken, and she relaxed.

"Oh, I know you will try to get me to join your prayer time, Lucu," she said, "but I don't believe in God. I don't think He exists. Or, if He exists, I don't believe that He cares or is a good God. And I don't want to hear about God."

I replied, "Well, I don't want you to participate in our prayer group because I don't want you to teach the youth to think like that. So, you can come with us, but please stay away when we pray and sing."

"Deal!" she said immediately. "Usually, people try to convince others to come. But you promise you won't invite me!"

"In fact," I said, "*If* you come to sing or pray, I am going to ask you to leave."

"Deal!" she said again.

"Deal!" I replied.

"Kum Ba Yah"

We arrived in the mountains after a whole day of traveling. When we got off the train, we paid a wood-hauling truck to carry us part way up the mountain. But we still walked four more hours to reach where we would camp.

We were so tired. We opened the food, ate, and pitched our tents.

Then someone said, "Let's pray and go to sleep."

As soon as she heard that, Elena disappeared into her tent.

I told the kids, "Let's start a bonfire."

"Where? Where is the best spot?"

"In front of her tent," I answered.

"Why?"

"Let's just do it," I said.

Soon the wood was burning, and we gathered around—right in front of her tent. I began singing, and everyone joined in.

"Kum ba yah, my Lord, *Kum ba yah."*

Zip! Elena poked her head out immediately. "You said you will not invite me," she accused.

I said, "Did anybody invite you? Go back in your tent!"

Now she was angry. She pulled on her boots and stomped around, taking down her tent. It took her about half an hour. Then she moved further away and pitched the tent again. This took another half hour.

Once she was inside, I said to the kids, "Let's move the bonfire." We moved it in front of her tent and started singing again, "Kum ba yah."

She came out in disbelief. "*Why* would you do that?"

"Hey," I said, "go back in your tent and leave us alone!"

She said, "You're preaching in front of my tent!"

"Move the tent," I said.

"I just did!"

She could not go back down the mountain alone. And she was too tired to move again. So she went to sleep.

The following day, she calmed down and came on the hike with us. But that night, we did the same thing. We sang and prayed and talked about Jesus' sacrifice, His love, grace, and transforming power, right there, in front of her tent. Next night, the same.

"I put two pillows over my head," she complained, "but I can still hear you."

I said, "Hey, you don't have to believe it. If you disagree, it's okay. We're not going to ask you to come to pray with us or believe what you hear."

She just glared at me. But every night, she heard us.

Do People Change?

The messages I shared were about transformation. "Let's start with a question," I said to the youth. "Do people change? Are *you* trying to change? How do change and growth really happen? Is righteousness possible? How can we be saved?" We talked about total dependence on God. We specified that it is our natural tendency to try hard to change. But, while we may change our external behavior, we will never be able to change our nature.

Every night, I gave a few examples from the Bible, like Mary, Zacchaeus, and the woman at the well. I shared how Jesus told Nicodemus that change is possible only through the Holy Spirit. The Holy Spirit brings conviction, repentance, salvation, transformation, fruit, and everything related to spiritual growth.

A few days later, Elena came to me so angry. "What you say is all a lie," she said. "People don't change. I've tried. I've tried hard to quit smoking and drinking, but I just keep going back to that scene. I prayed, and God *never* gave me deliverance. People don't have the power to change. Stop lying to these young people."

I said, "You are right. And you need hearing aids. I never said that *people* have the power to change. In fact, I said that they *don't* have the power. But *God* can change them."

She just looked at me. "If this is real," she asked, "then why can't I change?"

People don't have the power to change.
You may change your behavior for a while
but you cannot change your nature or your heart.

"Listen," I answered, "let me tell you what my dad told me when I tried to change my anger."

That's the Wrong Question, Son

When I was young, I was stubborn and proud. For some reason, I could do whatever I put my mind to—good or bad. I always succeeded.

Except I never managed to control my temper. I asked my dad, "How do I get victory over anger? How do I change?"

"You don't," my father answered. "That's the wrong question, son. You say, 'How do I change?' But it's not about changing your behavior. You *want* to be a patient man, so you try to hold everything inside. But an angry man who tries to control his anger is still an angry man. There is poison in the spring inside. You cannot change that. You may manage to control your temper for a while, but you will get angry again unless Jesus changes your heart. Only He can do it. You must be born again."

We cannot *make* the fruit of the Spirit. It is not *our* fruit. It is the fruit *of the Spirit*. Therefore, instead of trying to produce the fruit of the Spirit, we need to seek the *presence* of the Spirit. We must *have* the Spirit.

Only the Spirit bears the fruit of the Spirit.

We need times of dedicated prayer for God to pour the Holy Spirit's love and power into our hearts. Only His presence in us can transform us.

An apple tree doesn't produce apples to deserve to be an apple tree. An apple tree bares apples as a natural result.

We don't do good deeds to *deserve* to be a Christian. We *become* Christians because Jesus loves us and because we are forgiven and saved. We focus on Him and what He has done for us and seek a close relationship with Him. And when Jesus lives in us, fruit follows naturally with no human effort.

First, Jesus lives in us. Then we bare good fruit as a result. That is the order.

Back to Elena

"You're just like me," I told Elena. Then I quoted from the book *Steps to Christ*. "In like manner you are a sinner. You cannot atone for your past sins; you cannot change your heart and make yourself holy. But God promises to do all this for you through Christ. You *believe* that promise. You confess your sins and give yourself to God. You *will* serve Him. Just as surely as you do this, God will fulfill His word to you. If you believe the promise,—believe that you are forgiven and cleansed,—God supplies the fact; you are made whole."[1]

She started to cry. "What shall I do?" she asked.

"*God* promised to do the miracle of new birth in you," I answered. "Basically, He doesn't fix you—He makes you new. He doesn't fix a broken heart. He replaces it. He'll take your stony heart out and give you a new heart of flesh. And that's a creation miracle. Only a Creator can do it.

"If you decide to trust in Him," I continued, "then He will work with you. He has patience and mercy beyond human understanding. Don't try to make sense of how He works. Don't try to deserve it. Don't try to pay for it. And don't try to do it on your own."

"But how will I know if I am really born again?" she asked. "Especially if I cannot feel it?"

"God's work is not based on your feelings, Elena. It's based on His character. Take His word for it. He is able, and He wants to do it. Just say, 'Lord, I don't understand, but I'm going to decide to trust in Your promise, let You work, ask for Your presence always, and surrender daily.' Say that prayer every day," I continued. "Do not wait to *feel* you are made whole. Just say, 'I believe.'

"Keep your eyes on Jesus, not on yourself, not on your sins or problems," I told her. "Stay connected and trust in Him. Do not allow yourself to doubt His power or love. You don't need to understand how He works to believe. You will never understand it. Just exercise faith by saying, 'I trust in His love and promise. He gave Jesus for me, He promised to finish His work in me, and I am going to decide daily to trust in Him.' "

What we say influences what we think. We cannot allow ourselves to talk about doubt or think about doubt. Say, *I believe.* Not because you feel something but because Jesus promised, and He cannot lie.

***"We must talk faith, sing faith, act faith, and then we shall see the deep moving of the Spirit of God."*[2]**

"Jesus told Nicodemus that the Holy Spirit is like the wind," I said to Elena. "We don't see the wind; we only see the effects while the wind passes by. But change takes time. I've never seen a kid going to medical school one day and becoming a physician the next day. The same with this. I don't see people spiritually growing one day, and boom!—instantly, they are holy. It's a long process, and God has patience with us. We might not have patience with ourselves, but His patience is beyond understanding. What matters is that you ask Him, today and every day, to come into your heart and to work with you. It is a process. And as long as you are in the process, as long as He is in you, working with you, you are safe. Not because you deserve anything but because He is working on you (Col. 1:27)."

I continued, "Why don't you try out what I said on a trial basis? Pray and study every morning, surrender every day, exercise faith every day, and see what God does. Try it out. If it doesn't work, just drop it."

And she said, "I am willing to do that."

Transformation

Elena started to pray and study. She started to come to church every Sabbath. She was baptized. She went to university.

About six months later, she came to me and said, "When I started to study the Bible, it became air to me. I could not live without it. When I started to pray, it became more important than food. If I miss a day, I don't function. I love it—it is my life. It gives me strength. It gives me peace."

Today, Elena is married and has a family of her own. She is strong in the church—humble, kind, faithful, and spiritually profound. Her life shows the total transformation that comes from prayer through the power of the Holy Spirit.

". . . No man can empty himself of self.
We can only consent for Christ to accomplish the work.
Then the language of the soul will be, Lord, take my heart;
for I cannot give it.
It is Thy property. Keep it pure, for I cannot keep it for Thee.
Save me in spite of myself, my weak, unchristlike self."[3]

" 'I will give them an undivided heart and put a new spirit in them;
I will remove from them their heart of stone and give them
a heart of flesh.' " Ezekiel 11:19 (NIV)

[1] Ellen G. White, *Steps to Christ*, 51.
[2] Ellen G. White, Letter 50a, 1898 par. 5.
[3] Ellen G. White, *Christ's Object Lessons*, 159.

SUMMARY

God promises that if we allow Him to be our God and have no other gods, then *He* will change our hearts. We cannot do it.

Yet, so often, we try to monitor ourselves. This is just what Satan wants. He knows if we keep our eyes on self, we will become discouraged.

And a fully discouraged Christian is a fully useless Christian.

But God says to keep our eyes on Jesus, the Captain of our salvation.

Growth is a process. From being a spiritual baby into the fullness of Christ—it takes a lifetime.

Change happens through faith. By faith, we trust in God and allow Him to work. By faith, we believe and are transformed by His Spirit in us.

He says, "*I* am going to give you a new heart. I am going to give you a country that is not yours. I am going to give you gardens you never planted. I am going to give you homes that you never built. I am going to give you victory. I will do it *all* for you."

7

CHAPTER

I DIDN'T LIKE YOU, EITHER

When I was young (not that I'm old now!), I got too many ideas. Thousands of ideas. Many of them about playing pranks. I never missed an opportunity to play jokes on people.

At school, I'd put grease on car door handles. At church Sabbath mornings, I'd be in the balcony looking for people who seemed to be sleeping. Then I'd shoot grains of rice out of a straw at the back of their head. They would jump and put up their hand to where the rice hit. This was very funny to me.

Some of my targets complained to my mother nearly every day with warnings like, "He will *never* change."

Of course, she loved me—so this both concerned and frustrated her. She'd say to my father, "Honey, what should we do? Should we discipline him?" Then I would hug and kiss her, and she would just melt. "Oh, you are so sweet, Lucu." But she'd turn right back to my father. "What are we going to do with him, Pavel?"

My father would smile and give me a hug. "I did it, too," he'd say. "God loves a challenge, and your mother and I are praying for you, Lucu. God changed me, and He will change you, too. Can you imagine when God is going to use this creativity and energy for *His* work? I know He'll do it because we pray day and night. Right now, you don't know God so well because you are young. But you know us. Through our actions, we want to show you the grace that God is showing to us so that you will know God through us."

A Step Too Far?

I remember one time when I thought I might have gone too far—even for my father. It was the winter of my seventh-grade year. The communist education system held classes six days a week. Those who didn't go to school on Saturdays would often be punished, sometimes mocked by the teachers, or even expelled. My math teacher especially didn't like me. She would continually call me names, put me on a bench away from everyone else, and try to make me fail my exams. Our French teacher was different. Professor Andrei was young, tall, and athletic. He told jokes and laughed and even sang with us sometimes. He also wore a big Texas-style hat.

One afternoon when school finished, my friends and I ran outside shouting at each other as we grabbed up snow. A tall narrow pole with a flood light stood near the school entrance. Our favorite game was throwing snowballs at the pole. We'd back up further and further, seeing who could score the most. I had a strong arm and was very competitive. I usually hit the pole dead center.

I was about twenty meters away, stepping up to take my turn when the front door opened, and Professor Andrei walked out. I saw that tall hat and could not resist the temptation.

"Hey, everyone," I called. "Who thinks I can hit Professor Andrei's hat from this distance? It's a moving target! Who wants to bet I can knock it off?"

If it had been *any* other teacher in the entire school, I wouldn't have dared. But it was Professor Andrei. He might say, "Drop and give me ten," but I knew he'd secretly enjoy it.

Everyone watched as I took aim and threw as hard as I could. That snowball launched like a rocket. It could not be more perfect! But right then, Professor Andrei glanced over. In a split second, he saw the projectile winging toward him and ducked. My snowball flew over his hat and crashed into the window behind him. Glass shattered. Everyone fell silent.

I was ordered back inside the school while my father was summoned. I kept wondering what he would say. Would he be angry? Most of my pranks were little compared to this one. I had destroyed public property.

Father arrived and spoke with the administrators. Then we headed home. He still hadn't said much to me.

Mother was waiting at the door. "Lucu! How could you do this, honey?"

She turned to my father. "Pavel, what are we going to do about these pranks? He needs to stop doing it. You always say, 'he is just like me,' but this time, he is *not* just like you!"

Father hung up his coat and looked at me. "You're right," he said finally to mother. "This time, he is not just like me."

I felt my stomach drop. But father was still speaking.

"This time, he is *not* just like me," he continued, "because *I* would have hit the hat." He grinned. "There's the difference between you and me, Lucu—I would have managed not to miss!"

"Pavel!" my mother protested. "How can you joke? Should we discipline him?"

"Honey," he answered, "don't we all deserve discipline? Look how gracious Jesus is with us."

Then he hugged me. "My father forgave me, Lucu, and we forgive you. Just as Jesus forgives us, so we forgive you. Now, this is how we will fix it. First, we are praying for you. As for this window, you and I will go and fix it together. You have to work to pay for it. You come with me next week to work, and whatever you earn, I'm going to match the amount. Then I'm going to take time off and help you replace the glass. Whatever you need to do, I will do it with you. We will fix it together because your mother and I love you. And also because you cannot do it alone."

Do you know how much I loved my parents for how they worked with me? The way they showed me God's love?

My parents taught me about grace by the way they treated me.

We, Christians, aren't always comfortable with grace. We don't understand it. We feel we must somehow earn it. Or at least pay it back with good work. But the thief on the cross paid nothing for grace. And he died before he did anything good. We cannot purchase grace. Period.

In one of Jesus' parables (Matt. 18:21-35), a man who owed 10,000 talents of gold said to the master he owed, "Forgive me, and I will pay you back." The servant is offered forgiveness as a gift, for free, by grace. Yet he says, "Forgive me, and I will pay you back." That doesn't make any sense. If you are forgiven, there is nothing to pay back. Your debt is gone. And if you pay a debt back, you don't need forgiveness because you earned it. You paid for it.

That's how we often feel about asking God for forgiveness. We are tempted to mix His undeserved grace with our merits and works. Do works have any place at all in our life? Indeed, they do. But not in order to earn or deserve salvation. Any good work comes as a natural result of Jesus living in us.

Grace is *undeserved* favor. Grace is an *unearned* gift. The servant in the parable receives *free* forgiveness. When we are forgiven, there is nothing to pay back. Our debt is gone.

But if we do not accept God's free gift of grace, then we also have no clue how to show grace to others. We must grasp the magnitude of grace and receive it before we can share it.

Please note that I am not talking about enabling the one who did wrong to keep doing it. Jesus gives clear biblical boundaries in Matthew 18:15-17 to prevent continued harm and sin. However, we still must receive God's grace and show it to others. We call ourselves Christians, but we often don't know how to be like Christ—forgiving and compassionate to those around us.

We cannot give grace to others
unless we have received it ourselves.

Without grace, our prayers will be selfish prayers. We will not genuinely care for others enough to intercede for them. We only will be able to extend grace by the same measure that we receive it.

Alvin

Alvin was a member of a church I pastored. He was arrogant and got furious if anyone dared to oppose him. He was also rich. We're talking *really* rich. He constantly tried to control the church with his money.

Other members warned me about him before I even preached my first sermon. "Pastors don't last here very long," they told me. "As soon as you have any type of conflict with Alvin, he will start fighting you. He will call and write the conference until they move you."

I remember how Alvin took me aside soon after I arrived. He pointed his stubby finger at me, almost putting it on my nose. "Young man, you don't know me, but you'd better learn to listen when I talk. In this church, we do things a certain way. If you do what I say, you'll have a good life here. If you try to do something different, you'll be gone."

I quickly learned that none of the members argued with Alvin, either. If they did, they would lose. No one would oppose him because he had too much power. And in time, they got used to that.

Things between us bumped along for a few months as I grew to know the church. Alvin wasn't entirely thrilled with me and always managed to find something to pick on in my sermons. But we didn't hit any major potholes.

Until a budget discussion arose one night at a board meeting.

Alvin decreed that the church would spend enormous money on an item we could not afford. It would take all the money literally in our church savings account. One of the members timidly asked how we would be able to pay our regular church budget items, like utilities.

Alvin sneered. "I give this church the money—and I say where it gets spent. If you do not approve this, you will never see another penny from me."

Now I spoke up. "I think we all need to share our thoughts. We can discuss this together and see what others on the church board think."

Alvin flushed slightly. Everyone else sat silently. I looked around. Nobody would meet my eyes. Nobody had any courage to stand up to him.

"Come on," I encouraged. "Does anyone have any questions?"

One lady finally said, "I wonder how we can repair the roof leak over the primary room if we buy this?" Other members began adding in their concerns. Alvin grew more upset, and the debate became more heated.

"Why do we have this argument?" I finally asked. "We have simple rules here. We talk about it with kindness, and then we vote. Then that vote is what we do whether we personally like it or not."

"Young man," Alvin shouted, "I *am* the vote here."

I continued, "Why don't we vote privately. I will give everyone a piece of paper."

Alvin glared at me. "You'd better get out right now," he said.

"Why?"

"Because I make the rules."

"But the vote is for everybody, not just one person," I said calmly.

"You obviously don't know what you are talking about," he said, clenching his hands.

I said, "Listen, folks, we need to pray. If God inspires you that our church should make this purchase, vote 'yes.' If He inspires you not to make this purchase, then vote 'no.' But vote what God puts in your heart."

We prayed and took a secret ballot. For maybe the first time in forty-eight years, Alvin was voted down. He surged to his feet and strode toward the door, saying, "I am going to teach you *all* a lesson." The door slammed so hard that the windows rattled. Then it immediately opened again. "And *you* are stupid," he raged at me. "You don't know whom you're fighting with."

"Don't call me, or anyone else, 'stupid,' " I answered. "If you do it again, I will have you put out of the meeting because you don't respect people."

I thought Alvin would explode. He grabbed his cell phone and called the Conference president right on the spot.

"How much budget do you still need for your academy dorm construction project?" he asked.

We could clearly hear the president's voice. "Good evening, Alvin. We still need over 1 million dollars." Of course, the president had no idea what was going on.

"I will pay the whole amount if you will move Pavel Goia to another district." It actually made me feel strangely satisfied—no one had ever offered so much on my head!

Now the Conference president got the picture. "No, Alvin," he said. "I can't do that. You need to learn to respect your pastors and work with them." That made me feel very good.

Alvin's voice rose. "You'll never get money from me again," he said, shutting the phone.

Hatred, Lies, and Misery

From that time on, Alvin made my life miserable. He criticized my sermons every week. He didn't care who overheard the criticism, either. He berated me at every turn.

He often called the Conference office to complain, twisting every word I said. One time I preached about having a relationship with God. "Keeping the Sabbath is good," I said. "But it doesn't help to keep the Sabbath if you don't have a personal connection with God through prayer and reading His Word."

Alvin called the Conference. "He said we should not keep the Sabbath," he reported. "He said that it's not important."

The president called me on the phone.

"I did not say that!" I defended myself yet again. "I would *never* say that. I will send you a recording of the sermon to prove what I really said."

The president sighed. "You don't need to send the sermon, Pavel," he told me. "I believe you. Just keep praying. I know Alvin can be difficult. This is your challenge; see if you can find a way to work it out."

The attacks and lies continued. Week after week. I grew discouraged, then angry, then bitter. I dreaded preparing sermons or attending board meetings because all I could think about was how he would criticize my words or go against me at every step.

"I'm going to end your ministry soon," he would often say as he walked past me at the door.

For many weeks, I would come home and cry. I got stomach pain. I was not able to eat.

Ask Yourself

Now, let me ask you a question. How do you treat that type of person who constantly hurts you, makes your life miserable, calls you names, and lies about you? Not for just a day or two, but month after month?

How do you treat someone who wants to destroy your life? Someone who doesn't care that you have a family, children, or a ministry?

After months of vicious attacks from Alvin every Sabbath, every board meeting, every church event, I felt exhausted. I continually prayed for God to resolve things and help me, but there was no answer.

"I am so worn out from all these battles defending myself," I told Daniela. "I don't have anything left for ministry. Just think what our church *could* be doing if I didn't always have to deal with Alvin."

Then Daniela said something I will never forget. "Remember how your parents worked with you when you gave them so much pain and headaches. You need to do the same with him; you need to show grace. What if God put you here specifically *for* Alvin?"

"What? NO! He will never change," I said, forgetting how many people used to say that about me.

"Then maybe God put *him* here for *you*, and *you* need to grow," Daniela answered. "Unless you learn this lesson, how can you be a pastor? Let's start praying for him."

"I *am* praying! I've been praying for months."

"Well, you are not praying for *him*. You are praying for *you*. You pray that he will stop bothering *you*. That God will help *you* and solve this problem. To you, Alvin is just a problem. But what if you invest time praying for *him*?"

"I will not. He will never change," I repeated.

Daniela reminded me that we cannot expect grace unless we share grace. That we cannot expect forgiveness unless we also forgive. That we don't understand and appreciate God's love unless we love others.

"Remember, Jesus commanded us to love even our enemies. To the degree you love Alvin, to that same degree you love Jesus," she said. "Stop trying to change him," she added. "You have no right to change anyone unless you are willing to die for them. Pray that God would change you instead of asking Him to change others around you."

So Daniela and I started to pray for Alvin.

In the beginning, I could not even say his name because I resented him so strongly. I prayed, "Lord, I don't like this man. But you said to pray for our enemies. So, Lord, help this evil guy."

Daniela gently corrected me. "You need to say his name in prayer."

I knew she was right. "Okay," I agreed. "Lord, help Alvin. I don't want to see him lost. I cannot imagine how I will ever love him. But I want him in heaven, so please turn Alvin around and save him."

I thought that was a pretty good prayer.

Daniela said, "No, that is not enough. Didn't Jesus give up His life for His enemies? You need to say, 'Lord, take *my* life and save *him*.' "

"*You* say that!" I retorted. "I cannot."

But Daniela went right on. "Didn't Moses say to take his name off the book of life—eternal life—if God would not save the Israelites who tried to stone him?"

"Yes, Moses did say that. But I am no Moses!"

"Didn't Paul say, 'I would rather be *anathema*—cut off—from the book of life if they could be saved'?" I wondered how long Daniela's list of examples was.

"I don't have the strength to do it," I told her.

"Pray anyway," she answered.

So I tried. "Lord, I would really, really, *really* like You to work with Alvin. But I'm not sure I am willing to say these words like Moses and Paul."

Then God spoke in my mind and said, *You will never be a Christian before you are willing to lay down your life for somebody else, including your enemies. You cannot be My follower unless you do what I did.*

He didn't say, *You'll never be a pastor.* He went further than that. He said in my mind, *You will never be a Christian.*

I started to cry. "Lord, help me to be like Jesus. Fill me with love so I will not criticize Alvin even in my heart. And not just that I don't hate him, but I pray for You to save him even if You lose me!"

That was a tough prayer to pray. I had a hard time even saying it. But after I said it, I had a peace that I could not explain.

Yet, nothing got better. Has that ever happened to you? Does it ever seem that the more you pray, the worse it gets? I was tempted to stop praying, but we continued. Daniela and I did not give up.

When we start to pray, God starts to work.
But things don't always get better right away.
Satan wants to discourage us so that we will stop praying.
Don't give up. Keep praying until you get an answer.

About a month later, I realized that I wasn't having stomach pains anymore when I saw Alvin. Instead, I felt peace. I felt confident that God was there, giving me strength; He was working.

Even though nothing changed in the situation, the most amazing miracle happened in my heart. God changed my thoughts about Alvin. He took away my stony heart. For the first time, I began to really care about Alvin. I really wanted to see him in heaven. The more I prayed for him, the more I *really* desired an answer to my prayers. Not for my sake—but for *his* blessing. God gave me a new heart for Alvin. God gave me His compassion. His love.

Hope with God

One night, we got an urgent telephone call. "Alvin had a heart attack today. They've admitted him to the hospital. Surgery is tomorrow." I drove over right away. Daniela said, "Make sure you stop on your way and get a card and some flowers to brighten his hospital room."

I was not ready to spend my money on someone who hated me, so I got a cheap bouquet.

When I walked into his room, Alvin was alone, staring out the window.

"Why are you here?" he asked, surprised. "Get out. I don't want to see you."

"I came to see you and pray for you," I answered.

"I don't need your prayers," he spat back.

"I got you flowers and a card."

"Give me those." As soon as he got hold of the flowers, he whacked me over the head with them. There were flower petals and leaves all over the floor and bed—some stuck in my glasses and hair. "Get out," he said sternly. I cannot describe the feeling in my stomach.

I went home very sad. I said to Daniela, "I see no results of our prayers in Alvin."

She said, "Expect great things when you pray and keep praying as you would pray for your own family."

I kept visiting every day. Even after surgery, his prognosis wasn't hopeful. His attitude toward my visits never changed.

Then one day, Daniela made cookies. Scrumptious Romanian cookies that still make my mouth water when I think of them.

She said, "Take some cookies when you visit Alvin tonight."

When I walked into his room, I said, "I have some cookies for you, but please do not throw them at me. If you don't eat them, I will. They are wonderful."

"I don't want your cookies. I want nothing from you. (pause) But they do smell amazing. Are they good?"

"Oh," I said, "they are the best in the whole world."

"Let me taste one." He "tasted" all of them within a few minutes and didn't even offer me one.

"Why do you keep coming?" he finally asked. "Don't you know that I hate you?"

"To be honest," I said, "I didn't like you either. But I thought about what Jesus said when He asked us to love even our enemies, and I asked God's forgiveness for not loving you. My wife and I now pray for you every day. And I would really like to pray with you, too."

"Don't bother praying for me," he said. "It's too late. The Holy Spirit left me years ago."

"How do you know?" I asked.

"When I was young, I sinned a great sin. Plus, all of my life, I have done too much damage. I've hurt too many people. At times, I convinced myself that I was doing enough good things, giving lots of money to the church, and doing things for the church to win God's forgiveness. But I've caused too much pain. I don't deserve forgiveness or salvation. I don't see how God can forgive me."

"Oh, my brother," I said, "we *should* obey God, serve His church, and give to Him because we love Him. However, when you talk about God's love and grace and forgiveness, all of the bad things you've done don't matter. And all of the good things you've done don't matter, either. God forgives you because Jesus died on the cross for you. He paid for you in full. He died for sinners. His blood covers the sin of the whole world. And His grace is sufficient for any sin, regardless of how big or how many."

"I did ask forgiveness a hundred times, but He never forgave me."

"Brother," I said, "you asked ninety-nine too many times. The first time when you asked Him to forgive you, with a broken and humble heart—in that very moment, He forgave you."

"But I never felt like I was forgiven."

"You don't feel forgiveness," I told him. "It is not like electricity. You must take Jesus' word for it. It is by faith. The Bible says that He forgives and cleanses us if we confess our sins (1 John 1:9). Period. It is God's promise, and God doesn't lie. It is very simple. It's not feelings; it is a mental decision. You choose to believe God's Word, and you rejoice in it. At that moment, you are forgiven."

"Do you really think there is hope for me?" he asked.

"Yes, yes, yes!" I said. "Listen, do you want to be saved?"

"Yes! But how do I know if the Holy Spirit left me or not?"

"Your question is proof that the Holy Spirit did not leave you. Satan just wants you to think that so you will have no hope. But you *want* to be saved—and human nature does not want to go back to God. Human nature wants to run away. But the Holy Spirit put in your heart the desire to go back to Him. Just like the Holy Spirit told the Prodigal Son, 'Go home. Your Father loves you. Go back.' "

"What should I do?" he asked.

"You need to confess your sins," I answered. "And then you need to believe that you are forgiven."

"Is it really so simple?"

"Absolutely," I assured him. "Salvation is simple. Children get it because it is simple. Adults look to complicate things, and they don't get it."

Right there, he closed his eyes and said, "Lord, forgive me of my sins. All of them. Will You please forgive me? Amen."

He looked at me. "Do you think I am forgiven?"

I said, "For sure, you are forgiven! Jesus promised forgiveness, and He is faithful. Now you are as white as snow. Jesus took all your sins upon Himself and, right now, He gave you His perfect divine robe of righteousness."

"But what about the people I've hurt?" he asked. "Shouldn't I confess to them, too? Will you help me?"

Over the next few days, as Alvin grew weaker, I spent hours by his bed, helping him dial and hold the phone so that he could apologize to people. He was a changed man. Humble, kind, full of joy and hope.

Alvin didn't leave the hospital alive. On my last visit there, he looked at me with tears in his eyes. "Pavel," he said, "God brought you here for me. I probably would not have changed at this stage of my life. I like control. I like to be in charge. Never would I believe that God could forgive me. But He sent you to show me His grace. He brought you here for me," he repeated.

I told him, "Brother, God put *you* here for *me*. I did not know how to love some people. It's easy to love those who love you. But God put you here for me so I would learn to love those people I do not get along with, to pray for them, and show God's love to them."

The next day, Alvin slipped to rest, knowing he was forgiven and saved because of grace. I look forward to seeing him in heaven.

Miracles still happen today. Especially miracles of grace. Grace that transforms hearts. Grace that transforms relationships. Grace that transforms churches. When God's presence fills our hearts, His grace is naturally manifested to others.

Praise God for His unbelievable, incredible, infinite, amazing grace.

SUMMARY

"The ground of all forgiveness and grace is found in the unmerited love of God, but by our attitude toward others we show whether we have made that love our own."[1]

Do you know how much you love Jesus? To the degree that you love the one who hates you and makes your life miserable. To that exact degree you love Jesus. "Assuredly, I say to you, inasmuch as you did *it* to one of the least of these My brethren, you did *it* to Me" (Matt. 25:40).

God is calling us to pray for those who hurt us—those who left a scar. Because He loves those people.

We can never do this in our own power. But as we keep our eyes on Jesus, on His cross, on His love, the more we will grasp the depth of His forgiveness and grace for us and the more we can extend grace to others.

God put us here for them.

[1] Ellen G. White, *Christ's Object Lessons*, 251.

CHAPTER 8

I WANT TO SLEEP

One Sabbath evening, I gathered my last energy to preaching one more time. I'd been speaking all weekend in a prayer conference and was exhausted.

The day before, I left my home at 4:00 in the morning to drive to the airport. After layovers and delays, I landed at my destination twelve hours later. The first meeting started in less than two hours. I had no time to check into my hotel and freshen up. I went straight to the church.

In twenty-four hours, I spoke at six different meetings. Friday night, Sabbath School at 9:00 a.m., and church at 11:00 a.m. Then, after potluck, another seminar at 2:00 p.m. Then again at 4:00 p.m. No time to breathe, no time to rest.

After I finished the final meeting at 7:30 p.m., we had a Q&A session that lasted quite a while. I felt ready to collapse.

But instead, I had to rush back to the airport to catch the 11:00 p.m. red-eye flight home. I was dead tired! I felt like a lemon being squeezed during back-to-back meetings like these. And I was losing my voice, which usually makes my wife, Daniela, quite happy!

All the way to the airport, I kept praying, *Lord, please help me. Please let nobody sit on my left or my right. Please let the whole row be empty so that I can sleep! I want to sleep. I am so drained. Please help me.*

I made it through security. When I boarded the plane, I began to feel really hopeful. People kept walking past me, and the seats stayed empty.

Lord, please don't let anybody sit next to me, I repeated every time someone approached my row, just in case He had gotten distracted and forgot.

And then God spoke in my mind. *Remember what you preached.*

I began thinking back on some main points. *God and His plans should come first. We must walk with God and be always ready to listen, ready to serve, ready to forget ourselves, and put God and His plan first. We must make ourselves continually available to God's leading and be light—be salt. We must sacrifice ourselves and be a blessing to others, like Jesus.*

God asked me, *Is your prayer for empty seats for you—or Me?*

Well, it's for me. But I'm tired!

Who gives you your health?

You do.

Then why do you worry about sleep? Shouldn't you put Me first and let Me worry for you?

You Could Lose Everything

My thoughts went back years earlier to a similar conversation with the Lord. I was facing a final hydraulics exam in college. If I failed this exam, I would fail the entire year.

This was the kind of exam to really stress over—lots of math and physics. In our classroom, blackboards covered the front and the back walls. We would have to fill those boards with equations, proving how a dam would not break under the pressure of a storm or earthquake with the right elements—concrete, steel, torsions, etc.

I planned to spend the day before the test reviewing my entire textbook so it would be fresh in my mind. God woke me up early that morning, and I started to pray. I'd learned from my dad always to say, *Lord, help me seek You first, above all other things. Help me seek Your plans, Lord. I want to be connected to You—available to You. I want to serve you. I want to forget self and be filled with Your presence until I am with You and You are in me.*

As I finished praying, my phone rang. It was someone from the church. "Hey, Pavel, we need your help. Can you come?"

My first tendency was, *No. I have a final. I must finish the entire book. I cannot. I need to use every second.* But then I thought, *I prayed for God's plan. What if this is God? But what if I go to church and then get so tired that I can't even manage to finish the whole book later?*

I heard God in my thoughts. *Who gave you school? And who gave you your health? He can help you with the exam too. Are you willing to put Me above your school? Would you be willing to give up school for Me?*

So I decided that God came first, and going to the church to help was His will. I was happy to surrender my school and put God first. I then had peace.

Surrender is a lifelong process that happens daily.

I went to church and spent basically the whole day helping. But my day was gone—no more time to study. I managed to review part of the book and then fell asleep.

The following day, I prayed and went to school. As I began reading the questions, the answers immediately rolled through my mind. Formulas were flooding out as I wrote. My memory was so fresh—everything was coming back.

We had four hours to finish the exam, but I finished in less than two hours, including bonus questions. The grading scale was one through ten. To advance in education, you needed an eight or higher. I remember the teacher giving me my score: "10+," he said. "Congratulations."

Once again, God showed me that even when you sense you might lose everything, you must put God first, and He will provide for you. You must be willing to surrender *all*.

We don't lose anything when we follow God and His plan.

Lord, I Repent

Now, I sat on the airplane having the same talk with God as I asked Him to keep the seats beside me empty so I could sleep.

I heard Him again in my thoughts. *Haven't you been preaching that you should walk with God and be ready to sacrifice self for Him and His plans, that you must have an open ear and an open eye to His voice and leading? Be open to the opportunities He gives you to serve? Be ready to surrender your plan and seek God's plan?*

Yes, Lord, but I need to sleep. I need to recharge. And then a powerful quote came to my mind: "Christ in His life on earth made no plans for Himself. He accepted God's plans for Him, and day by day the Father unfolded His plans. So should we depend upon God, that our lives may be the simple outworking of His will."[1]

We usually seek God's blessing for our plan.
Instead, we should seek God's plan, and then we get His blessing.

As I settled on the plane seat, I thought, *Lord, okay, I repent. I surrender my focus on self, my focus on sleep. I am happy to give up my sleep, ready to follow Your plan. If You have somebody in great need, put them next to me.* Be careful what you pray for!

As soon as I thought that, a lady wearing a huge puffy parka climbed over me to sit on my right by the window. She moved all around as she settled and took one-third of my space. I leaned away as far as I could.

While she was shoving her overflowing quilted carry-on bag under the seat in front of her, another lady in a thick wool coat wedged herself into the seat on my left. I wondered if they thought we were going to Antarctica instead of Atlanta.

I could not move. They squeezed me like a sardine in a can. I thought, *Lord, come on!*

Now I was kind of a little unhappy. *After almost six hours in flight, I will be numb*, I complained silently. I decided to put on my headphones, listen to the Bible, and try to sleep.

But the lady by the window started to cry. She put her head in her hands, her shoulders shaking.

And right away, I realized, *Wow! The Lord put her next to me because she needs a blessing.*

I said, "Can I help you?"

"Just leave me alone!" she snapped.

"Okay." But she kept crying.

The lady to my left said, "How can you help her?"

"Well, I don't know. I could pray for her."

She brightened up. "You believe in prayer!"

"Absolutely!"

"I do, too!" And she started talking. I was tempted to interrupt her and give her a lesson on prayer, but you should never talk before you listen. So I let her talk, then I shared a few things. I focused on giving her a story related to prayer rather than the theology of prayer. Stories are non-threatening, and they go straight to the heart. They also allow the Holy Spirit to bring up the lesson needed for the listener. We had a pleasant conversation about prayer for maybe half an hour or more.

Meanwhile, the lady on my right stopped crying and started to listen. Then she spoke up. "I'm sorry I was rude. But regardless of how much you pray, it's not going to change my situation!"

"Well," I said, "what is your situation?"

"When I got on the plane, I got a text from my husband telling me he left me for another woman. What can God do about that?"

I didn't answer immediately because Jesus says in John, "I don't speak on my own authority. The Father who sent me has commanded me what to say and how to say it" (John 12:49, NLT).

So, instead of answering the lady, I said, "Give me a second."

And, just as Nehemiah prayed before answering the king, I prayed in my mind, *Lord, I cannot help this lady. Her husband left her. What can I do? Please, You promised that those who ask for wisdom would receive it. You give with a large hand, God. Give me wisdom after Your promise. I am not asking for myself. I am asking to be a blessing for her.*

God loves unselfish prayers.

And He gave me words at that moment.

I then said, "Right now, it is hard. I cannot imagine what you're going through. But it's going to be better. What I'm about to say might be a little strange, but please listen. People don't just stop instantly loving someone—your husband stopped loving you years ago. First, he stopped talking with you. Then you started to have conflicts, and he treated you in a way that was not right. There was no more care, no more respect, no more patience. Just more and more pain. He started to cheat on you long ago and didn't dare tell you. Tonight, he decided to say he was leaving, but that is just him expressing what he has been doing for a while.

"Also, I want you to think about this," I continued. "When you go home now, no one will be screaming at you. You don't need to worry about when the next fight will be. It will be tough for a while, but you will find healing times and find peace. You will be able to start life all over again. And this time, make sure you start it with Jesus. Make sure you pray and involve the Lord in your next step in life. Because you don't know people, but Jesus knows people. And He is going to give you somebody who will love and respect you."

Her mouth fell open in shock while I was talking. "How do you know all these details? You are right! My life is exactly the way you said. But how did you know? Are you a prophet?"

"Nope!" I said. "But I prayed that God would give me the wisdom to comfort and encourage you, and He impressed me to say these things."

God Talks for a Reason

As I've said before, sometimes, when we pray for ourselves, God answers differently than we ask because He has different priorities. When we pray for others and make ourselves available to Him—that's a prayer He loves the most.

I remember once when my wife, Daniela, and I were driving from Tennessee to Wisconsin. It's usually an eleven-hour drive, but it was snowing, and the roads were slippery.

We were praying as we drove. We decided not to listen to music or news but instead pray and listen to the audio Bible. We didn't pray generic prayers—we prayed specific prayers. Generic prayers take seconds, and often we don't even need to think about what we say because they become routine. But when you pray specific prayers, it takes time. You concentrate and put your heart into them. They are like an honest, open conversation with Jesus. We prayed for our family, our kids, and the church. We started going name by name. All those who had challenges. All the church departments one by one. For the leaders. For our neighbors.

By now, we'd driven through Tennessee, Kentucky, and entered Illinois—almost halfway home. It was wonderful to be praying with Daniela. To have all these hours together as the miles rolled on.

Eventually, I came to my regular prayer, "Lord, I'm driving. It doesn't seem like I can serve You while driving through the snow but

Lord, if you can use me today for others—if You need me to serve You, then make me a blessing. Here I am. I make myself available to You."

As I was praying, my cell phone rang. It was one of my friends. He's a wonderful pastor who is always ready to help and sacrifice himself.

But I was praying with Daniela, and I didn't want to be interrupted—even though he is a great guy, he does talk a lot, often even more than I do! So I silenced the phone and said to Daniela, "I'm not answering right now. I don't want to get distracted. When do we have time together like this? Let's keep praying."

And I continued right on. "Lord, I make myself available to You. If you need me today, please let me know."

And He said in my mind, *I just did.*

O Lord! I thought right away. *I'm so sorry! I put my preference above You. I'm so sorry. Please fix it.*

And the phone rang again.

Daniela asked, "Who's calling you?"

I gave her the name.

She said, "He's a friend, but it always takes hours every time you talk together. It's better if you call him later. Otherwise, you will be on the phone for the rest of the trip!"

"But," I said, "we have been praying for God's plans, making ourselves available to His leading, ready to forget self and be used. What if this is God's answer?"

"Very well," she said. "Answer it, but keep it short."

"Hello?" I answered the phone.

"Hello," my friend said. "I'm just calling really quick to ask you to pray for me. I'm supposed to fly today for a mission trip. But I'm afraid I'm going to miss my flight. My car has broken down, and it is snowing so badly that the shuttle won't come, and no church members can take me."

He lived a few hours away from the Chicago airport in Illinois.

I said, "Brother, what exit off the highway do you live?"

He told me.

"Well, it happens that I'm driving up to your exit right now. Give me directions."

"What? You live in Wisconsin. What are you doing in Illinois?"

"We're driving home from Tennessee. How do I get to you?"

He said, "Take the exit, turn left, and drive straight for nine miles."

We picked him up and took him right to the airport in plenty of time. He went on his mission trip, and God blessed through wonderful evangelistic meetings.

The point is that God doesn't talk just to talk. He talks when there is a need. And we must always be ready, always listening, and always willing to forget self and follow His plan.

When We Got to Atlanta

Back to my airplane story.

"I can't believe you prayed, and God talked to you," the lady by the window said again.

Then she had a new thought. "I want to ask your advice," she said. "I'm in a lot of pain and stress right now. How do I get over it? How do I function and get it out of my mind?"

I said, "Well, I'm not a counselor. But I know that when I have a bad song playing in my mind and can't get rid of it, I play a different song. When I have bad thoughts, I think about something better. My advice to get rid of these thoughts and pain is to fill your mind with better thoughts. Fill your mind with prayer, study, service, and being a blessing to others. Focus on Jesus."

"Wow!" she said. "But how can I start to connect with Jesus?"

I opened my briefcase and took out my first book, *One Miracle After Another*.

"Here," I said, "take this book. Read a chapter. If you don't like it, give it back. If you like it, keep it!"

"But I never read. I just like to watch TV."

"Just read a chapter and then decide you want to read more."

"Okay," she agreed.

She read one chapter. Then she read the next chapter. And the next. She was laughing and crying. Sometimes, she'd turn and give me a hug.

When we got to Atlanta, she said, "I'm going to give this to my daughter to read. I'm going to give this to my neighbors. Now I realize that I need to be connected to God and live for Him." And she gave me one final big hug goodbye.

About a month later, she sent an email. "I wanted you to know that God put you next to me. I planned to go home, take a handful of pills, and end everything. God saved my life. He spoke to me through you. I started going to church, and I started praying. I believe it was not by chance that I sat next to you. I believe that God put you next to me. That flight, that night changed my life!"

When we make ourselves available—willing to sacrifice our plans and comfort—the Holy Spirit works miracles.

SUMMARY

Surrender is a lifelong process that happens daily.

Real commitment means a willingness to do whatever He wants us to do. To the degree we commit, to that very degree God can work in us and through us.

God's plan doesn't often appear easy. We might sense that we could lose everything if we follow it. But we will never lose because God can take care of our needs better than we can ourselves.

May we all seek Him each morning, saying, "Lord, give me opportunities today to serve. Teach me not to be so focused on myself that I don't hear the voice of the Holy Spirit. Open my eyes. Here I am. Send me, Lord. Use me."

[1] Ellen G. White, *The Ministry of Healing*, 479.

CHAPTER 9

THAT WAS ONLY THE BEGINNING

"Pastor, we don't believe in evangelism here. We have tried. We spent money. We lined up good speakers. It just doesn't work in this city."

I received this information during the first board meeting at my new church. God had clearly led Daniela and me to a wonderful active congregation *full* of good, caring people. If a member ended up in the hospital or faced a difficult situation, someone would soon visit them, and others would organize food delivery. These were dedicated hard-working folks. But they'd had a hard time with outreach.

Another member spoke up. "We've tried to give Bible studies. We've held seminars. And nobody came." Then another spoke. "This city is very affluent. Half of them are extremely rich. The other half go to other churches and believe they're already saved. There is no way to do evangelism in this city. It may work in a different place, but not here."

Very strange, but you hear the exact words in many places, "Evangelism doesn't work here." Then where does it work? Evangelism is not a human invention, and it is not a suggestion. It is Jesus' command. If it doesn't work, can it be that we just need to revise how we do it?

Pray Big Prayers

My new church clearly had a history of disappointments. It was easy to see why they were so skeptical. Right away, Daniela and I began to pray. I remembered what my father said, "The way you win is through prayer."

So we prayed together for God's plan for this city. Every morning from 5:00 a.m. to 7:00 a.m., we prayed. You may wonder what to say when you pray for so long. If you pray generically like, "Lord be with my church," that takes only seconds or minutes. But prayer must be specific.

For instance, don't just say, "Forgive my sins." You must name your sins. Don't only say, "Thank You, Savior, for Your blessings." You must name your blessings. And we should not forget any of His blessings.

"Bless the Lord, O my soul, and forget not all His benefits."
Psalm 103:2

Daniela and I prayed specifically for each church member by name—for each mother and father and child, for every family, their health, and their work. We prayed for the church departments and leaders by name. We also prayed for God's vision.

When you pray specifically, it takes time and commitment. Moreover, you start knowing each family, name by name. The more we prayed, the more we wanted to see answers.

Daniela and I declared war in prayer. Too often, people pray anemically—they don't put their heart into it. But they still expect God to work.

When you pray small prayers, you get small answers.
But if you want big answers, you need to pray big prayers.

A major way to change anything is to pray. And you must exercise faith. Pray big and expect an answer. Praise the Lord in faith for what He will do. We did not pray for just a day or a week. We were determined to pray until God answered.

Many times, in the Bible, answer to prayer is not an event but a process. When God answers, He has a different plan than we do. And He answers so big that we often cannot comprehend it. You need to keep praying. Meanwhile, God works with you and the others, preparing everyone for His plan. Prayer connects you with the source of all power. With God, everything is possible.

The disciples were given an impossible task. They were a handful of people with no money, no media, and no resources. They were asked to evangelize not just a church, city, or their country but also the whole world. They knew they could not do it in their power. But Jesus promised to give them the Holy Spirit.

We have noted before that, in the Great Commission, Jesus did not first say to go to the whole world and preach the good news (Acts 1:4-8). He said to remain in the city. Basically, do not attempt to do God's work in your power and methods. Wait and pray. The disciples must have wondered how long they should wait and pray. But Jesus did not give them a time limit. Instead, He asked them to pray *until* they received the Holy Spirit. When you receive the Spirit, then you shall receive power (v. 8a). Then go.

Jesus says that whenever two or three pray together in one accord, it shall be given to them (Matt. 18:19). Praying together in unity of purpose is something that God really loves. The disciples knew their total dependence on God. They prayed together for the fulfillment of His promise for the Holy Spirit. And God answered.

Daniela and I were determined to pray for our church. And that takes time. God had to work with us. We had to pray enough to make sure that we would obey it when God gave us His plan. And God had to work with the members and also with the city. And that takes time and many prayers. It takes commitment to prayer.

We prayed *for* them, and then we prayed *with* them. Besides praying for them early in the morning, I started to call a few each day and pray with them for their families and their needs. I also started to preach and teach about prayer. And not just on one Sabbath, but for several months until the church became a more praying church. A praying church is a church where God leads.

Camp Meeting Miracle

For three months, nothing happened. So we kept praying. I also set aside every Monday to pray in the church building for God's plans. I'd spend the whole day praying over every chair, every room, and even in the parking lot, asking the Lord to fill that place.

Soon it was camp meeting time. I love camp meetings because you get to meet with people. At the same time, I also don't like camp meetings because you pitch tents that are old, dusty, moldy, and full of spiders. Pastors always go early to help set up. That Monday, I was pitching tents.

I prayed for the church and God's plan as I pitched the tents, trying to avoid the spiders and dust. What should we do to grow? To reach the community? To fulfill our mission? What would work in this city? I prayed that prayer all day Monday.

Instead of going to bed on Monday night, I decided to pray that whole night. I said, *Lord, I'm not going to let You go before you tell me what the way is. I will be like Jacob. I will grab You. Either You kill me or give me the solution.* And I prayed with humility and determination, with faith in God's promise.

Eventually, in the middle of the night, I fell asleep kneeling on the floor with my head on my bed.

God woke me up early—way too early in the morning. Around 2:30 a.m. It wasn't a voice saying, "Wake up!" Instead, He woke me up with a bunch of thoughts. *This is what you do in this church.* I found a pen and started writing down all the steps that God put in my mind—step one, step two, and so on. Lots of picky details. My father used to say, "Whatever you try just to remember, you forget. Whatever you write down, that's what you remember." So, I wrote it all down. It took a while, but I filled four pages.

How do you know when God talks? When He talks, it is not much connected to what you would logically or usually do. And it is often not very comfortable. I *knew* these were not my thoughts because they had nothing in common with what I usually did.

I also knew the church would *never* logically agree with this plan—it was too big. It would involve a lot of time, energy, and work. It wasn't an evangelism *event*—it was a year-round evangelism *lifestyle*. I thought the conference *might* agree with it, but I also knew it would be unlikely for them to offer financial support. Everyone would say, "We don't have the people. We don't have the money. It's too much commitment."

So just like King Jehoshaphat put the list in the temple—I put my list before the Lord on my bed. I said, *Lord, if You gave me these thoughts, I need two things: I need Your confirmation that this is Your plan, and I need Your promise that You will support it.* I kept thinking, *God, I'm not going to let You go. If this is You, I need to know.*

I prayed for confirmation up until breakfast time. Breakfast is a holy time for me—like Sabbath and family time. I don't miss a meal. I said, *Lord, I've got to go eat*. But I continued praying while I got ready.

Then the phone rang. It was a wonderful man who had previously been my teacher. "Good morning, Pavel! You asked me to come to speak about church growth at your new church about four months ago. At that time, I told you I wished I could come, but I was already booked for the entire year. Well, I now have a Sabbath available. But I want to speak about something different. We've done some surveys, and I want to suggest a new approach to evangelism. We would like your church to try this project. Let me tell you about it."

And he told me the same basic points that I had written down on four pages of paper after praying! I was speechless. "Are you there?" he asked.

I said, "Wow! I have been praying for God's leading in my church for months now. God woke me up this morning and gave me thoughts. But when I looked over them, I said, 'This is too much! I need confirmation.' And what you just told me now are the same steps that God gave me one by one. He just confirmed it."

He said, "I'm coming to your church to share the plan! God is going to do great things!"

Telling the Church Board

I went to my board and told them the whole story but not the plan. I told about the months of praying with Daniela. Praying through the night on Monday. God's answer and four pages of details. The call of confirmation.

They were excited. "Wonderful! What did God say?"

"I'm not going to tell you," I answered.

Everyone was shocked.

"This process is going to be different than what you usually do," I went on. "It is a *life-changing* vision. I want you to receive it from God so that you will truly support it. If I tell you, it may be too difficult to accept it, moreover to do it. You need to pray until God prepares you for His plan and gives you the vision. Then you will certainly do it.

"So here's the deal," I said. "You go home and pray for a month. Ask God to prepare your hearts and minds. Ask Him to give you faith. I want you to ask the Lord to give you the vision. And then we will do it together."

And they all agreed. "Okay, Pastor." They all knew the value of prayer. For that entire month, I called members every day, a few each day, and we prayed together, and they also prayed alone.

At our next meeting a month later, both our head elder and our Bible study coordinator said, "Pastor, we sensed that God gave us an idea.

It's not for thirty days of evangelism—but for *much* more. Evangelism should not be an event but a way of life, an ongoing process. We need to reach the community. We need to hold seminars so that people come to the church. We need to conduct Bible studies to expose people to the gospel before they come to evangelism."

I said, "This is it! You touched the principles!" And everyone was willing. "Let's do it!" they said. Then I gave them the rest of the details. They were all excited and hopeful.

The most crucial idea, which is not new, was that evangelism is not an event but a way of life; it is not for a week or a month, but for the whole year, each year. And not for one area of the church's life but every single one. You cannot expect to go into your garden and pick up tomatoes if you have never planted any. You must prepare the ground, plant tomatoes, water and weed them, and so on.

Here's a short summary of the basic parts of the plan they all agreed on and began to implement:

1. Develop a consistent environment of prayer for and with all leaders and members in their personal lives and in the church. Prayer was a vital part of the planning, the activities, and the outreach of the church. Everything was immersed in prayer.
2. Preach and give seminars focused on prayer, spiritual growth, and mission.
3. Give Bible studies using professional audio/visual materials. Members focused on building relationships with people they gave Bible studies to rather than preparing and teaching the studies.
4. Hold mingling and caring activities for the community for over three months. For instance, invite the police force and firefighters to the church for a meal and pray prayers of blessing and protection for them, visit hospitals and nursing homes and pray for the workers and patients there. Clean parks, feed the homeless and pray with the people.

5. To build relationships and trust, sponsor felt-needs seminars at the church, such as cooking classes, "stop smoking" classes, depression recovery classes, and many more. After a few seminars, visitors will feel comfortable in the church facility and build rapport with the members.
6. Conduct public evangelism once a year, preceded and followed by 40 days of prayer.
7. Follow-up with new members on structured discipleship. Call weekly and visit new members monthly by an elder or a deacon. Involve them in prayer groups, a special pastor's class, assess their gifts, and get them involved in an area of the church where they can use those gifts. Encourage them to give Bible studies to others (this activity helped secure them in the church).
8. Repeat and improve yearly.

What were the results? The church attendance almost tripled. The members' involvement went from an average of 15% to about 85%. The baptismal retention rate rose to 80% or more. We gave around 200-250 Bible studies a year. We started a radio station and had several hours a week on local cable TV. Visitors would regularly say that this was the most praying and friendly church they had ever been to. These are just a handful of results. There was a strong sense of God's leading and presence.

After the Walk in the Forest

A while after the set-up of the evangelistic plan, Daniela and I began inviting the whole church or leader groups to our home on several occasions. We would eat around a bonfire, sing, share, play games, and pray for one another—for our church and our community.

Once when a leader group came over, after we sang and worshiped together, I said, "I know we have been praying a lot for God's leading for a while now. Let's now focus on what God wants to happen in our church for the next five years. I want you to each take a walk in the forest and pray. When the Lord tells you about what should happen, come back. But don't come back before God tells you. Now go into the forest and get busy praying. Do not come with your plans. Our God is a big God—a God of the impossible. Our small plans limit Him. He has no limits. Pray for His plan and then trust in Him. We usually seek God's blessing for our plan instead of seeking His plan. When He gives the plan, then He gives the blessing."

Everyone smiled and headed out. One hour or more went by. People were coming back. One by one, they sat around the bonfire until everyone returned. They were very quiet. Very sober.

"Pastor," one of them commented, "what God put in my heart is *big*."

Everyone wrote their vision for the church on pieces of paper and gave them to me to read. As I glanced through the papers, I felt dismayed. I couldn't believe what I was seeing.

"Friends," I protested, "I asked you to pray for a vision for how our church can reach the community. But you are going far beyond that. You are way too broad—way too large, too big; this is too much. Look at all these things you write: 'Media ministry,' '24/7 radio station in two languages,' 'meetings and seminars for the community at least six times a year,' 'everyone giving Bible studies,' 'mission trips,' 'evangelism with worldwide impact.' 'Seminars with worldwide impact,' 'canvassing every year,' 'access to local TV.' We cannot do all of it! We don't have the people to do all this! It is too much, too big. And we don't have the money."

"But, Pastor, didn't you say the vision should be big because we have a big God? Didn't you say that when God gives the plan, He provides the resources? You told us to pray in faith, and God would bless it."

"Yes, He will bless it," I said, "But this is too much. Let's pick two or three things from this list–things that we can do."

"No. We want everything. We prayed seriously. God told us. Now we want you to help us do it."

"Listen, folks. We pick only three. Period. I am your pastor."

They were very discouraged. But they stopped arguing because they loved me.

I was relieved because I wanted them to start with something manageable. Something we could build on slowly. Not something unrealistic, like canvassing the whole city—we didn't have enough people to do that. Or their idea for a *radio station*. That was a *huge* project. *Far* beyond our budget. To buy all the necessary equipment, to cover twenty-four hours a day, seven days a week. Where would we *put* the equipment? We had no space even to house a radio station.

Of course, I knew they were disappointed when I limited them to only three options. But I also knew they would eventually understand I was right—that it was much better to start with something small. Something we already could handle.

The Broken Cell Phone

The next day, I flew to a conference where I was to preach about prayer. Yet, after speaking the first night, I felt unable to pray. I was struggling inside. I couldn't sleep very well. I felt no peace. I prayed, *Lord, if there is something between You and me, You need to tell me, and I will confess, ask forgiveness, and fix it.*

In my thoughts, He answered, *You asked the people to pray. I gave them the vision, and you opposed Me. You sent them into the forest to pray, but you did not pray. Instead, you worked in the kitchen preparing the meal. The plans they provided were from Me, and you are the one opposing the vision instead of supporting it.*

Right away, I felt so sorry. *O Lord, forgive me. I will go before the church. I will confess my mistake—but please fix it! I need You. I'm really sorry. I know You forgive me, but I also need Your help. I ask You to fix it because You love me. And You love the church. And those people are not at fault.*

Then I went to check my email. As I started to open my laptop, I accidentally knocked over a cup of water on the desk. My mobile phone was next to the cup, and it got completely flooded. That was the end of my phone. It was utterly destroyed. Gone. Dead. I took out the battery and dried everything with a hairdryer. I put it in a plastic bag with rice. I put it back on the phone and tried to turn it on again and again. Dead. No screen turning on. I even prayed for its resurrection, but no miracle happened.

I borrowed another person's phone to call Daniela.

"Hey, honey," Daniela answered, "I miss you. Why didn't you call me on your phone?"

"I destroyed my phone."

"Praise the Lord. You will now stop giving me a hard time when I break my phone," she said. She had a tendency to drop and break phones, and I'd always tell her, "I've never broken a phone in my life." Now, it was my turn.

"Even though you can't call me on my dead phone, I will borrow a phone and call you every day," I assured her.

After I returned the borrowed phone, I went back to my room. *Lord, again I am sorry. You gave everyone this long impossible list as a vision. It seems too difficult. We will need so many resources. And so many people. But would You please not only forgive me but also help me and fix my mistake? I want to do whatever You say.*

My dead phone started ringing.

"Hello?"

"Pastor Pavel, I am not a member of your church, but I live nearby. Some time ago, God put on my heart to start a radio station. But my church is so small, and your church is larger and more active. So I want to offer you everything we have—the building, some money for the equipment, the tower—everything. We will donate it all to your church if you are willing to start a radio station."

I was stunned. I couldn't believe it! When we said goodbye, I tried to call Daniela on my previously dead phone and tell her the good news. But my phone was still broken. Dead. Finally, I put it down and kept thanking the Lord for the miracle of the radio station gift.

Suddenly, my dead phone rang again. It was the Conference literature coordinator.

"Hello, Pavel," he said. "You told us that your church wants to do canvassing every year. We are going to work with your church for free. We will send students from the academy and provide the books. There will be no expense to your church except to give them food and lodging."

Then the phone rang again! The lady on the other line said, "I am the general manager from the local cable TV. I have been listening to some of your seminars online, and I think they would be a blessing to our city. We need good programs in our city to provide spiritual and emotional support. I am offering you four hours of free programming time every week if you want them."

"Praise the Lord!" I said. After that call, my phone was still dead. In fact, it never worked again. But God was starting a *huge* work. I'd just received a little glimpse of the miracles that would come in years ahead.

The next Sabbath in church, I stood up. "Folks, I have to confess. I have sinned. We prayed. God gave you a vision. And I got in the way. I am sorry." Then I told them the miracles He was already doing.

But that was only the beginning.

SUMMARY

My father used to tell me, "When you start praying to be filled with only God, and when you begin to know Him, and hear Him, and follow Him, He works beyond your imagination. Your prayers are too small because your vision is too small. The human mind cannot see how God will work."

But when people get together and pray, things happen.

CHAPTER 10

GOD HATES BLUE EYES

When God first sent the vision for our church to begin a radio ministry, it seemed impossible. We had no equipment and no space to house it. We prayed about it and were strongly impressed that it was God's leading and vision. "Lord, if this is your plan, we know You will provide the means. We ask for Your help. We need the space and the equipment."

We kept praying. In time, God impressed a faithful member from a different church to donate the location and all the equipment we needed, including the huge radio tower.

All we needed to go forward was a radio permit from the Federal Communications Commission (FCC). The approval process included a hefty fee when we submitted our application.

I gave the church three months to raise $24,000 for the paperwork. The very next week, we had over $56,000. When God comes, money and resources come.

The problem we often have is not a lack of money—
it's a lack of God's presence!
When people sense God moving,
when they see God working,
they support it.

In any endeavor, we must never go alone. We must always make sure the Lord is with us. Like Moses, we should say that unless God goes with us, we will not move from here. And when He is with us, He will provide the means.

Soon we faced the next potential roadblock—getting approval for a frequency from the FCC. The opening paragraph on the FCC site shows how real that obstacle could be.

Potential applicants for radio and television services should be aware that frequencies for these services are always in heavy demand. When application filing window periods open for new stations, many competing applications are filed. Filing an application does not guarantee you will receive a broadcast station construction permit. In many areas of the country, no frequencies may be available on which a new station could begin operating without causing interference to existing stations, a violation of FCC rules. For that reason, we do not recommend that you purchase any equipment before receiving a construction permit from the FCC.

At the time we applied, there were four frequencies available in our area. But *sixteen* institutions were applying. Frequencies were awarded using a scale of points based on how well your station served the community. There was a chart used to determine your point level based on various value options, like offering emergency weather alerts and so on. Whoever had the most points held priority for approval. But if your application was rejected, you could not re-apply for many years.

We prayed for approval a lot. Jesus promised that if a few people pray together with unity of purpose, agreeing in prayer, He will answer

(Matt.18:19-20). We prayed together and unitedly for approval. We sent in our paperwork and fee. We were excited even though we knew there were many others with higher priority.

After all, God had already blessed so much. We were excited; we had momentum. We couldn't wait to see what He did next.

In June, we received a letter from the FCC. Our application was rejected.

We did not have nearly enough points. Many other applicants with more points were rejected, too. We weren't even *close* to the amount necessary.

Discouragement filled everyone as the news spread—it felt like a funeral. Now we had to wait several years before we could apply again. "We thought God was leading," people said to one another. "We thought He gave us the vision, the location, and the equipment. Maybe it was all just in our minds. Maybe God wasn't really with us. Otherwise, why would He allow this?" They were so confused, so sad.

I said, "No, no, no, no, no! We cannot doubt God when we face a hiccup. In the Bible, nothing goes easy when people follow God. Satan attacks. If Satan doesn't attack, we need to wonder if we are really following His plan. God allows trials to increase our faith and for us to know that it was Him working and not our doing. He wants us to acknowledge Him and not take credit for ourselves when the problem is solved. It is God and God alone. We deserve no credit. God allows this because He has bigger plans than we do. We just need to keep praying."

I continued, "As we look into Bible history, every single time God led His people, every time they faced challenges and attacks, that was no reason to give up. But, rather, to pray more. The greater the attack, the greater the need for prayer, and, therefore, the greater God's intervention will be. For instance, God led Israel out of Egypt. The Egyptian army came after them. That was a real crisis. However, that should have been no reason to doubt God's plan or leading. Instead, it is an opportunity to pray more and experience His amazing intervention. People who get discouraged and give up praying and working give up faith. They lose the opportunity to experience God's power. They have no story. Let's keep praying."

"Okay, Pastor." And we went on praying.

In August, we received another message from the FCC. "You have been previously notified that your application was rejected. Please withdraw your application."

"No," I told the board. "Do not withdraw the application. Leave it there and keep praying."

"Pastor, you do not understand. The law is the law. There is nothing more we can do."

I said, "We cannot have big miracles without big challenges. It's natural to want big miracles with small or no challenges. But the people in the Bible with powerful stories went through big challenges with big prayers. There is no story unless we have big challenges. Do not withdraw the application. God gave us the vision and the resources. He will take care of the approval."

"Okay, Pastor." We did not withdraw the application. We just kept on praying. August, September, October, November. Praying.

In the middle of December, we received yet another letter from the FCC.

They wrote that the machine used back in June to calculate the number of frequencies available had not functioned properly. It had somehow improperly stated that only four frequencies were available. Now, the FCC discovered they had five frequencies. Since everyone else who had been rejected withdrew their applications months before (even those who had more points than we did), our application was the only one left. By default, the fifth available frequency went to us.

You should have seen the celebration when I told the church members about it. "Just think," I told them. "If the FCC had seen this fifth frequency back in June, we would not have received it—they would have given it to the next one with more points. There were so many ahead of us that we would never have gotten it. But see how God works. Even when things don't seem to go right, He is still working, still in control!"

When God talks and leads, He provides! We got the vision from Him. He provided all the equipment. And He provided the approval. Our radio station went on air twenty-four hours a day, seven days a week, in two languages.

The Back Door

Step by step, God fulfilled the vision He gave us. In addition to the radio station, we started broadcasting on local cable television four hours a week, reaching our community. We also put our sermons on the internet. Eventually, about 400,000 people watched them every month from over eighty countries. Visitors started coming to our church. The whole church was like a beehive buzzing. We could see God working; His presence was visible.

People praying everywhere, working, excited and happy, and praising the Lord for what was going on in our church. There was momentum. There were stories. God's presence was felt. We all knew that He was among us and that He was working. I could write a whole book about the blessings of God on our church during those years. There were so many stories and proof of His presence and work among us.

But let me tell you one more story about the power of prayer. We made a rule in our church that we prayed with everyone who came through the door. Visitors said, "This is the friendliest, most loving, praying church we have seen." Everywhere you looked on a Sabbath morning—in the foyer, in the hallway, in the sanctuary—you would see people praying together before the service started.

But one Sabbath morning, a lady came in the back door while I was preaching and slipped into the last pew. Her hair was blue, red, purple, green—a kaleidoscope of color. There were rings in her eyebrows, rings in her ears, nose, and all over her hands.

As soon as I finished the sermon, I saw her slipping back out the door. Since all the church members were singing the last song, they did not even see her. Only I could see her from the platform.

I left the pulpit right in the middle of the song and ran down the aisle after her. I don't know what the church thought.

I saw her across the parking lot and sprinted after her. She was just reaching her car when she saw me coming. "I know you're the pastor, but I don't want to talk," she said.

"Okay. Then I will talk."

"I don't believe in God. Leave me alone."

I knew if I said, "Oh, please believe in God," I would get nowhere with her. I would never convince her—she had to convince herself. I needed to shock her and make her argue with herself.

So, I said, "You are drunk."

"What? I am not drunk."

"Yes, you are."

"No, I am not. Why do you say that?"

"Because you say you do not believe in God, but you came to church. Why would you be in church if you don't believe in God—unless you are drunk, missed your destination, and walked in by chance?"

She laughed a tiny bit. "I get your point. Okay. I *do* believe in God, but I just don't believe in prayer. So don't offer to pray with me or try to convince me to trust in God."

I knew she was expecting me to say, "Oh, yes, God answers prayers. Please let me pray for you."

Instead, I said, "I know why you don't believe in prayer. It's because you have blue eyes. And God hates blue eyes. He turns away from people with blue eyes. If you had brown eyes, like mine, He would hear you when you pray, but God hates blue eyes."

Her mouth fell open, and she said, "That's the craziest thing I've ever heard. And you're wrong. God answers any person's prayer regardless of the color of their eyes. He loves everyone."

I said, "Ha. First, you say you do not believe in prayer. Now you tell me that God answers every prayer. Make up your mind."

She laughed again and said, "Well, you cornered me."

I smiled back. "That's what I do best."

"Well," she said, "I guess I *do* believe in prayer. Theoretically. But I struggle. I don't seem to get any answer to my prayers."

I said to her, "Tell me what happened."

"I have been on drugs for sixteen years," she said, showing me the needle track marks in her arms. "Every two hours, I do drugs. If I don't, I start shaking and drop. I've been in jail, in rehab. I've prayed. God never answered my prayer. Over and over, I'd say, 'Lord Jesus, I am a drug addict. Forgive me and save me, please. I can't stop doing drugs. I love drugs. I am dependent on drugs.' And I keep confessing and asking forgiveness, telling God my problem again and again, with no answer."

"You're praying the wrong prayer, Sister."

"What do you mean?"

"You focus on sin instead of focusing on Jesus. After you confess your sin, God forgives you. That's a promise. If you confess, He forgives. Period. There's no need to confess it again. It's gone. The blood of Jesus is absolutely sufficient for you. The moment you confess, in that very moment, you are no longer a sinner. You are forgiven, righteous. Jesus takes your sin, and He gives you His own, perfect righteousness. So you no longer are in sin, and you should not focus on sin anymore. But it is not enough to be forgiven; you must also grow. You must get victory over drugs. And you cannot do it in your power; you need God's presence with you. When God comes in, Satan goes out; he then has no access to you.

"From now on, you need to focus on Jesus. Keep your eyes on Him; stay with Him. He says in John 15 that, separated from Him, we can do nothing. But if we remain in Him, we will produce much fruit. From now on, your goal is to stay with Him and focus on Him. You need to say, 'Lord, you forgave me, and I cannot change myself. But You have power. You died for me. You promised to give me a new heart. And I don't know how You will do that, but I know that You will because You are God. Please remain in me, live in me. I desire your presence. I want to thank You in faith, based on Your promise and love.'

"Focus on God, focus on His goodness, His promises, His power, and His sacrifice. Talk about *Him*. Don't talk about sin. Don't dwell on sin. Whatever your mind dwells on, that's what you do. You spend too much time thinking and talking about sin. This keeps your eyes too much on sin. You need to spend more time with Jesus. You need to keep your mind and eyes on Jesus, His power, His promises."

She said, "Okay. I never prayed that way."

"Well, it's time for you to start."

"What's going to happen?" she asked.

"You'll see. Let God work. He'll do what you cannot do. But there's another thing."

"What?"

"You need to give a Bible study."

"What? I don't know how to teach!"

"Wonderful! I don't want you to teach."

"So why would I give a Bible study? What is the connection with drug addiction?"

"You need to grow. You need to follow God's plans for you. God has plans for you daily, and as long as you follow His plans, you keep growing. The single way to grow is to serve Him, to follow Him daily. Follow His leading and plans. That's when He can work in you.

When you serve Him, you focus on Him. You stay with Him. You are busy working with Him. And, as you serve, you grow.

"God doesn't need us. We need Him. He has called us to work and serve because we grow closer to Him as we work with others. We learn to serve and love. As we teach others, we understand the Word better and better and become stronger spiritually. The more we serve, the more we get transformed into His image. The more occupied we are with sharing Jesus with others, the more we are filled with God's presence, and the less access Satan has in our lives."

"So, how do I give a Bible study?"

"Well, the first time, you knock on the door and do nothing because people are wary. So, just give them the Bible study guide and DVD and leave. If they ask why you didn't mail it, you answer, 'I want to make sure you don't confuse it with junk mail and trash it. I want to make sure you get the study.'

"The second time you go there, knock and say, 'How are you doing?' You give them the next DVD and leave. If they ask questions, say, 'I don't know. Don't ask me. I am not a teacher.' Do not teach; do not try to convince or change people. Just ask them to watch the DVD. I have never seen anyone normal arguing with the TV.

"The third time you go, pray for them."

"What should I pray?"

"Just say, 'God bless them, protect them.' And ask them what to pray for. If they have cancer or children on drugs, pray for God's presence. Whatever they ask for, pray about that.

"The fourth time, go in the house and watch the DVD with them. You must go inside their house. Your goal is to build friendship—to build a relationship with them. No one can lead a stranger to God, only a friend. Jesus did that too.

"It's not your job to convince them to accept God. That's the work of the Holy Spirit. Only the Holy Spirit can convince or change a heart.

When they finish watching the DVD and ask questions, just say, 'I don't know. Watch the next DVD.' And then leave."

"Well, I guess I can do that," she said. "But you're saying that if I give Bible studies, I myself will grow and get victory over drugs."

"Yes."

"What if I don't get victory? I'll never come back here if I don't get victory."

"Okay," I said. "Wait here." I ran into my office and picked a Bible study guide and DVD.

Coming back out, I said, "Now, here is an address of someone who asked for a Bible study. And here is the DVD and the study guide to give them. Bye."

She left. It was about 12:15 p.m. Fifteen minutes later, she called me. "Hello," I answered.

"I hate you," she said. "And I hate the church, too. I'm never coming back."

"Okay. Tell me why."

"Well, the address you gave me for the Bible study is an apartment building. You have to ring the bell, and somebody from inside has to open the door. I'm standing here ringing the bell, and nobody is home. God doesn't consider me worthy to give a Bible study and get me free from drugs."

"That's the reason you hate me? Did you pray that God would open the door so you could give a Bible study?"

"I didn't think about it."

"You need to pray."

"Okay." She hung up. A few moments later, the phone rang again.

"Hello?"

"I prayed, and the door didn't open."

"Sister, when did you pray? I didn't even have time to put the cell phone back in my pocket."

"Well, I prayed quickly!"

"That's not prayer. Small prayers bring small answers. You want big answers; you need big prayers. You need to mean it."

"Well, how long do you want me to pray? Five minutes?"

"Until the door opens."

"Ten minutes?"

"Until the door opens."

"One hour?"

"Listen carefully," I said. "Pray *until* the door opens."

"What if it doesn't open?"

"Then you keep praying. Pray until it is evening, and morning, and you get old and die praying.

"Now, if you prayed a petition prayer that God would give you a Mercedes or something else that you desire or need (I am talking about a temporary need), then you may want to put some limits to how long you keep asking God. Otherwise, it could look like you are trying to twist His arm. In that situation, you need to say, 'May Your will be done,' and mean that. Let Him make the final decision. He knows best what you need. He knows the whole picture and the future. You just need to trust in Him.

"But when you pray an intercessory prayer, that prayer is not related to temporary needs but eternal needs. That's when you are praying for someone's salvation. And that prayer needs to be persistent."

"Pastor, I'm not sure I can do it!"

"You have two options: Go back to drugs or start serving and let God change you and use you. Listen. I'm going to pray, too, while you pray. I'm not going to stop praying. I'll not eat, I'll not sleep, I'll not go home. When you call me that the door has opened and you managed to give a Bible study, then I will stop praying. So let's unite in prayer."

"Do you mean that, Pastor?"

"One hundred percent! Everything I say, I mean."

"Okay." She hung up again.

Five long hours went by. I was still in my office praying and so hungry. (Ring) "Hello!"

She was crying. "Pastor, you will not believe what happened!"

"Tell me quick, no introduction or much explanation. I am hungry! Give me the short story so that I can stop praying and eat something."

"I started out praying the nicest prayer my mom taught me, and nothing happened. Then I got upset. I opened my eyes and started arguing with God. I said, 'God, I know I'm a sinner. I know I don't deserve it. But would you open that door? I need to give a Bible study.' "

I told her, "Now you are praying! Prayer is not just words. Prayer is the opening of the heart!"

"Pastor, while I was talking to God, the door of the apartment building opened! A big tall guy with a ponytail and leather jacket came out carrying a trash bag to the dumpster. I stopped praying and ran over to him. 'Can you let me in?' 'Why?' 'Because I have to deliver a Bible study to Apartment 14, and they are not answering the bell. I'll just put it by their door.' He said, 'If they aren't answering, I am not supposed to let you in. And I am very frustrated with you!'

" 'Why? You don't even know me.'

" 'Well, I've asked for a Bible study before, and no one ever came.'

"So I said to him, 'Okay, you can have this one.'

"He said, 'But I don't know how to study. I've never studied the Bible, so come in and teach me.'

"I told him, 'No. The pastor said I just had to knock and give the DVD the first time.'

"He answered, 'Lady! You just offered me a Bible study. I've never looked at a Bible. I don't know how to study. You have to teach me how.' "

"What did you do?" I asked.

"I went into his apartment, and he told me to wait a couple of minutes and disappeared. When he came back, he brought several more people with him. All in leather jackets, some with ponytails. It seemed to me that they were a motorcycle gang. He said to them, 'Guys, last week at the bar, we talked about how all the drugs are killing us. Some of us have been doing them for forty years, and we need to stop. I went home and prayed for the first time in my life. I said that if there is a God in heaven, He should send an angel to help us give up drugs. And God sent an angel. Now, sit down and listen to her.'

"Pastor, I told them, 'I'm a drug addict just like you,' and I showed them my track marks. Then I said, 'Here's what the pastor told me this morning. I shouldn't focus on myself or my sins, but rather focus on Jesus, His forgiveness, and His power to transform.'

" 'The pastor also said that if I call on Jesus, He will work on me.' "

She was already preaching! She was on fire. She was happy and excited. "Pastor," she continued, "We started the Bible study DVD, and nobody moved for half an hour. Some of them started to cry. Big men crying. They said, 'This is the greatest thing we have ever heard. Can you come next week?' "

I will never forget what she said next. "Pastor, this is the best day of my life. So many times, I wanted to kill myself. Now I really want to live. And let me tell you the good news. I did drugs at 9:00 this morning. Now it's 5:30 p.m. I didn't do drugs for over eight hours, and I am not shaking. I don't have the need or the desire. In fact, I'm so on fire for God that I don't care about drugs!"

I told her, "As long as you pray and serve God and stay with Him, you are safe. He is with you. You need to stay connected. You need to keep praying and serving. As long as Jesus is with you, Satan has no room."

I asked her to come to church the next week to share her story.

She said, "I don't know how to preach!"

"No, it's going to be an interview. I'll ask you questions. It will be short."

On Sabbath, I brought her up front and asked her, "Do you know how to teach?"

"No."

"Have you ever spoken before a crowd?"

"No."

"Did you give a Bible study last week?"

"Yes."

"Was it difficult?"

"No."

"Did you love it?"

"It was the best day of my life!" And for the next few minutes, she shared the story.

I turned to the congregation. "How many of you want to give a Bible study?" Everybody raised their hand. Our church was visibly experiencing God's power. And the greatest miracle was not the radio station or any of the many other blessings. The greatest miracle was what was happening in the lives that were touched and the people that were transformed.

That young lady kept coming to church, week after week. I never told her to get rid of the rings. They disappeared. Her hair lost all of the bright colors. But her eyes are still blue. And she is still coming to church.

When people and church families decide to seek God's presence, to pray and follow His plan and vision, He becomes very real. He calls us all to a total commitment to know Him, walk with Him, and serve Him. You don't have to be a pastor. Wherever you are, whatever you do, God has something for you.

He has a plan and the means for that plan. You need to know Him and know His plan. You need to follow it and trust in Him. Make sure you have God's presence and leading, then the other things are provided. It is not about your wisdom, power, training, or means. Those are good and necessary things, but they bear no success without God's presence and leading. It is all about God, His leading, and power. It is not human planning but God's planning that brings success.

God says, "I know the plans I have for you" (Jer. 29:11, NIV). That is plural—plans—and it is present tense. It refers to today, every day. God has plans for you. It would be sad to call yourself a Christian and yet never know God's plans for you. To constantly go to God seeking His blessings for *your* daily plans instead of seeking to know and follow *His* plans.

I like these inspired quotes.

"Christ in His life on earth made no plans for Himself. He accepted God's plans for Him, and day by day the Father unfolded His plans. So should we depend upon God, that our lives may be the simple outworking of His will. As we commit our ways to Him, He will direct our steps."[1]

"If we plan according to our own ideas, the Lord will leave us to our own mistakes. But when, after following His directions, we are brought into strait/narrow places, He will deliver us."[2]

"Too many, in planning for a brilliant future, make an utter failure. Let God plan for you. As a little child, trust to the guidance of Him who will 'keep the feet of His saints.' (1 Samuel 2:9). God never leads His children otherwise than they would choose to be led, if they could see the end from the beginning and discern the glory of the purpose which they are fulfilling as co-workers with Him."[3]

"The reason why His professed people have no greater strength is that they trust so much to their own wisdom and do not give the Lord an opportunity to reveal His power in their behalf. He will help His believing children in every emergency if they will place their entire confidence in Him and faithfully obey Him."[4]

Do not fix your eyes on challenges but on Him and His promises. Seek His presence, seek His leading, trust in Him, and He will direct your steps. Make His presence and leading a priority, and He will lead you.

"Trust in the LORD with all your heart, And lean not on your own understanding; In all your ways acknowledge Him, and He shall direct your paths" (Prov. 3:5-6).

SUMMARY

God is inviting you to seek His presence continually, seek His plans daily, obey Him, follow Him, and trust Him fully.

Do not allow yourself to get discouraged. Remember, things didn't seem to go in the right direction for many of the Bible characters.

Even when you don't understand what happens around you, when things don't seem to go the way you would expect, follow His plan and leading.

1 Ellen G. White, *The Ministry of Healing*, 479.

2 Ellen G. White, *The Desire of Ages*, 369.

3 Ellen G. White, *The Ministry of Healing*, 479.

4 Ellen G. White, *Patriarchs and Prophets*, 493.

CHAPTER 11

TODAY YOU PAY, TOMORROW IS FREE

When I was seventeen years old, I planned the best Christmas program in the history of humankind—at least to my way of thinking. I was one of the directors of our adult choir at church and also directed our youth choir. I spent hours choosing songs. And weeks rehearsing the choirs. We had poetry and drama. We decorated the church with flowers and set up a special Nativity scene.

After the program, the whole church said a big "Amen!" and came up to express their appreciation. I acted very humbly, but I was as proud as a peacock inside. Later, I asked my dad, "Did you enjoy the Christmas program? Wasn't that good?"

My father responded, "Son, let me ask you a question. Who prepared the program?"

In my mind, I said *I did*. But I still wanted to appear humble, so out loud, I said, "*We* did."

"Who is 'we'?"

"We—the youth."

"What youth?"

"The youth of the church."

"And who was it prepared for?" he continued.

"For the church!" I answered.

"So," he said, "the 'church' prepared the program for the 'church'?"

"Well . . . yes!"

"Let me ask you another question. If you own a cow, and the cow makes milk, and then the cow drinks the milk—why do you have a cow?"

"What do you mean?" I asked.

"Son, you are not called to do mission in the *church*. Your mission is to the *world*. A farmer doesn't plant his crops in the barn; he plants them in the field and then brings the harvest *into* the barn. You are supposed to do the program for the world. But here, you worked in the church, not the field.

"Jesus sends you to *go* to *them*. Don't wait for them to seek you out. Do programs for the *community*. Then invite them in.

"If you prepare a song, then sing the song, listen to your own song, and applaud yourself and say, 'What a wonderful song we performed for ourselves!'—what is the benefit? Jesus called us to save the lost. Not to sing for ourselves, preach for ourselves, and then congratulate ourselves on the quality of our programs. He commanded us to *go*."

We, the church, are called to do mission.
We must do mission outside ourselves.

My father added, "Our mission is to tell the good news to the world. That work is *outside* the church. Remember, Jesus is coming soon." My father was not saying that we should not have choirs and have nice services for the church. We must, however, focus on sharing God's love with those outside of the church as well.

How Do We Prepare for the Second Coming?

Today, God is calling the church back to prayer, revival, and mission. A church is not healthy unless it serves and saves. And for that, we need prayer and the power of the Holy Spirit. The work will not close without that.

The work started in the power of the Holy Spirit, as the early rain. And the work will finish in the power of the Holy Spirit as the latter rain. The latter rain will be more abundant than the early rain. But only those who devote their lives to prayer will receive the Holy Spirit to help finish the mission.

When Jesus gave the Great Commission to His disciples and to us, He said to *wait and pray* for the Holy Spirit. Only when the Spirit comes will we receive power to *go and tell*.

We often talk about the Great Commission, but we don't seem to have a lot of results or much power. It seems impossible for us to reach the whole world. For that, we need God's intervention, His power. Can it be that we have not prayed enough for this?

My friends, God does not have a problem with the harvest—He has a problem with the workers. We have plenty of acceptable theories. Plenty of solid doctrines. Plenty of nice programs. But we need *true power* from the Holy Spirit. We need a *passion* for the lost. And we need to be *fully committed*.

As the Holy Spirit came at Pentecost in the book of Acts with results that were beyond human planning and imagination, so the Holy Spirit is waiting to come again, and the book of Acts will be repeated.

"Pentecost was introduced by the manifestation of Spirit of God in mighty power in the salvation of men and the extension of the gospel; the outpouring will come again with the manifestation of the same power, but in greater extent, to close up the work, and usher in the kingdom of God."[1]

God is working today just as in the past.

Miracle in the Mission Field

Years ago, when God gave a vision for service to a church I pastored, it included a mission trip to a communist country. We divided into three groups to go to three different locations without Adventist presence. We prayed that God would help us plant three churches.

For months, we raised money while we prayed. And God sent what we precisely needed to pay for the trip. He sent money for lodging, food, Bible workers, buses, and the rent to pay for the rooms in each location for the meetings. After that, we had enough money for the trip back home. That was all.

Our first night was amazing. I had twenty guests coming to my location. The elder at the second location doubled that with about forty people attending. But when I heard from the elder in the third area, the story was different.

They had welcomed about sixteen people to their rented building, and everything started well. Until the police came. They confiscated the materials, shut down the meeting, and told our elder that they would arrest him and his family if they tried to continue the next night.

"How could they do that?" I wondered out loud to the elder. "We got permits before we came."

"The police told me we only had permits from the government," he answered. "But they say we did not get local permits. So now we cannot keep going. Should we come and join you at your location?"

"Brother," I told him, "when we have challenges, it means we are doing what is right. And Satan despises it. When we have challenges, it is an opportunity to pray and experience God. So now, we will all pray. We will pray big prayers until we get an answer."

This elder, his wife, his children, and the entire team began praying. "Lord, we are not going to let You go before you help us plant the church. We came here to serve You and others—not ourselves. You have promised when we go that You will come with us. You promised that when two or three pray in one accord, You will answer. So, we are not going to move."

Around 2:00 in the morning, they felt at peace and went to sleep. The elder woke up the next day and heard God speak through an inspired thought. *Go talk to the police again.* He headed down to the police station, not even sure what he was going to say. When he got there, the police officer was not welcoming.

"You cannot continue with your meetings," he pronounced. "You do not have the proper paperwork. We will arrest you tonight if you go on."

"Can you please tell me what to do so that we can continue?"

The officer walked over and closed the door. Then he turned up the radio to cover their conversation. In a low voice, he asked, "Do you have any chocolate?"

"Yes."

"Do you also have a Bible for my family?"

"Yes."

"Okay. I will meet you at 2:00 p.m. on the corner. Bring chocolate for my family and me. Also, bring a Bible with pictures for my kids. And a real Bible for my wife and me. Put all this in a bag with something on top to hide it. Meet me at the corner, and I will tell you what to do. Don't tell anybody, or I will lose my job and freedom."

That afternoon, our elder met the police officer and handed over the bag of hidden chocolate and Bibles. The officer told him, "You cannot continue with your meetings in a *public* building. You need permits for that. *But* if you rent a church, then you can do them in a church with no permits."

Our elder thanked him and started searching. He then called me with an update. There were several different churches in town, and he had talked to every one of them. But no one would rent to him.

"Go back to the churches again," I told him. "Be like the parable Jesus told about the woman going to the judge. Keep going until they get tired of you."

"Okay, pastor." When he reached one of the churches a second time, their pastor said, "Since you came again, I will let you in with one condition. Our roof is broken. It will cost $2,500 to fix it. So, I will rent the church to you for $2,500."

The elder called me with the news. "Pastor, we have the envelope you gave us with expense money for our trip. There is $2,500 left for *everything*—food, lodging, transportation—everything is to come from this envelope. What should we do? If I give this all to pay rent, we don't even have enough money to buy our next meal."

I told him, "God is not going to give you more money before you spend what you have.

"Exercising our faith does not happen when we still have something but when we completely let go of everything and depend on God."

"Give the pastor the envelope in faith."

He called the pastor back. "We will pay you $2,500."

Praise God, the meetings continued that night! But the elder and his family did not eat. And they slept in their van since they couldn't pay for another night of lodging.

Before going to sleep, they prayed together. "Lord, thank you for the people who came to the meeting tonight. Please continue to bless them. And please do whatever you want with us. You know what we need. We want to forget self and serve *You* with full commitment. We will keep preaching and trust *You* to take care of us." Then the elder turned to his wife. "Honey, why don't you look in your purse? Maybe you have a little money there, and we can get something to eat." You know, you can find almost anything in a woman's purse!

When she checked, she found the original budget envelope with $2,500 still inside. "Oh dear, honey!" she said. "We forgot to give the pastor the rent money envelope. I still have it in my purse! We must call him first thing tomorrow."

Early the following day, the elder reached the pastor. "I'm so sorry we forgot to give you the envelope last night."

"What do you mean?" the pastor answered. "I'm holding the envelope in my hand. Everything's fine. You already gave me the money."

The elder hung up and called me. "Pastor! By mistake, you must have given us two identical envelopes with money. I paid the $2,500 rent, but we still have another envelope with $2,500."

"No, I gave each group their correct envelopes," I told him. "I am very precise."

"Then the angel of the Lord must have put this envelope in my wife's purse!"

The elder and his family ate a great meal and paid for a new hotel room. They slept very well that night.

The next day, they counted what remained in the envelope. There was $2,500.

He said to his wife, "You probably miscounted, honey. Maybe it was $2,800 before, and we spent $300 yesterday for food and hotel."

This time they counted together. Then they paid the bills for that day, too. The following day, there was $2,500. They gathered the team, and *everyone* watched as they counted.

The elder called me again. "Pastor, you will not believe it! We keep taking money from the envelope, yet the money does not go down. It's always $2,500 in the envelope."

I was not surprised. I know my God.

But I joked with the elder, "Give *me* that envelope! I would like an envelope like that!"

The elder laughed. "Pastor, there's a much bigger miracle than the envelope. The first night when I preached at the church we're renting, we had sixteen people again, just like opening night. Plus, the pastor and his family. But the next night, we had over 150 people! I asked the pastor, '*Who* are all these people?' The pastor told me, 'Well, I came last night and loved what you preached. So, I called my whole church and told them to come.' "

"Pastor," he said, "now I know why God took our original building. These people would have never heard the message otherwise. God wanted me to come to *them*."

On that mission trip, the three teams did a fantastic job. God blessed tremendously, many new believers were baptized, and three small churches were planted. The elder from that third location later told me, "I've been an Adventist my whole life. My parents and grandparents were Adventists. But I have never experienced *true power*. On this trip, I have learned what power is. I am not the same. My life has been changed."

"And we know that all things work together for good to those who love God, to those who are called according to *His* purpose" (Rom. 8:28). God is *longing* to pour out the power of His Spirit on each of us and His church. Christians have no power today because we are not fully committed, and often we rely more on our methods and plans and less on God's power. To the degree we commit to Him and His service, to that same degree will we experience God's help and power. For *full commitment*, we will receive *full power*.

"To everyone who offers himself to God for service, withholding nothing, is given* power *for the attainment of measureless results."[2]

The Crisis

On Friday night, March 4, 1977, my family came home from church and prepared for bed. We lived in an apartment on the fourth floor about 340 kilometers (211 miles) from Bucharest, Romania.

Suddenly, our whole building started to move violently from side to side. People began screaming and running down the stairs. A powerful earthquake (7.2 on the Richter scale) went on and on. Thousands were injured, and many lost their lives.

Furniture shifted in our apartment. The piano slid. Things fell off shelves, and we struggled to keep standing. My mother cried out, "Lord, if I have sins, please forgive them. We love You, Lord. May we all be saved!"

My father smiled and said, "Honey, don't wait for a crisis to pray like that. Do it every day!" Then he began to sing, "Rock of Ages, cleft for me. Let me hide myself in Thee!"

My mother asked, "*How* can you sing during an earthquake?"

He laughed. "I open my mouth, and it comes! A thousand may fall at my side and ten thousand at my right hand (Ps. 91:7), but if God wants us to be alive, we will be alive. If He wants us to die, we will see Jesus on the resurrection day. Praise the Lord!" Then he turned to us. "You have voices," he continued. "Let's sing! God is here. We are ready for anything."

We all started in again. "Rock of Ages, cleft for me."

The building was still shaking when someone knocked on our door really hard. We were so surprised that we stopped singing.

"During an earthquake, someone knocks on the door?" Father asked, crossing over to open it.

Two of our neighbors stood there. "Mr. Goia, can we come in?" the lady asked.

"Please let us come in," the lady repeated. "There is no safe place anywhere in the building except here!"

"Why would you say this is a safe place?" my father asked.

She answered, "We always hear you singing, my husband and I. When we fight and struggle, we hear you praying. When the neighbors are in need, you give them food and pray for them. We know that God lives in your house."

I will never forget the following words. "This is the single safe place in the building. Please let us in. Heaven is here, and everybody can see it!" My father opened the door wider. "Well, come into heaven!" he exclaimed. "You can sing with us. I will tell you the words."

After the earthquake stopped, my father prayed. Then he put one arm around each of the neighbors and said, "Friends, listen carefully. Don't wait for a crisis to invite heaven into your home. You need to invite heaven in *today*—and every day. Then when the crisis comes, you will not panic because heaven is already in your home."

Learn to Walk with God Today

Jesus is coming again—sooner than we think! We can't wait for the crisis to start preparing.

I say to you what my father said all those years ago. Every morning, we must commit our life to God. Every evening, we must confess our sins and believe His promise to forgive. We must seek His presence continually, abide in Him, and be filled with His Spirit. Daily we must surrender ourselves and our plans to God and seek *His* plans. We must make ourselves available for service. We must help others, show them love, and reach them for God. We must go and tell. We need to be so filled with His presence that heaven lives in us.

Unless we learn to walk with God today,
we will not walk with Him tomorrow.

God is calling His church to a new life with Him. He wants to fill us with His Spirit. He wants to start a revival in us that spreads all over the world like a fire. We cannot do that in our own power, but we can do all things in Christ, who gives us strength. He promised His Spirit to lead us in all things, and we must thirst for His continual presence in us.

Pray until you receive the Holy Spirit. Pray that God will keep you connected to Him. True power comes only through prayer. The center of our prayer should be God, His honor, and His work. The function of prayer should be a relationship—to know Him, get closer to Him, and be one with Him.

Spend time with Jesus. Pray continually. Pray when you drive, when you eat, when you walk, when you talk. Power flows through connection. And the single way to connect with God is through prayer and the study of His Word. Do not worry about how you will grow spiritually—seek His presence; that is your part. And He will provide the growth and the fruit through His Spirit. He promised that if you seek Him with all your heart, you will find Him. Spend time with Him.

All people of faith have been people of prayer. They walked with God, and they talked with God. They had His presence. They depended on His leading. To walk with God is to be continually connected. " 'Abide in Me, and I in you. As the branch cannot bear fruit of itself, unless it abides in the vine, neither can you, unless you abide in Me. I am the vine, you are the branches. He who abides in Me, and I in him, bears much fruit; for without Me you can do nothing . . . . If you abide in Me, and My words abide in you, you will ask what you desire, and it shall be done for you' " (John 15:4-7).

If you fall tomorrow and forget to pray, do not get discouraged; do not stop. Go back to prayer. Don't give up. If you fall next week and forget to pray, go back to prayer. Don't give up. The righteous will fall seven times and get back up (Prov. 24:16). Go back to prayer. Don't give up.

Pray for people. Pray specifically. Make a list of names. Be persistent, be intentional, and be precise. Don't be generic or anemic. You need to care if you want God to answer. Pray specific prayers.

Full Commitment

If there has ever been a time to serve Jesus, now is that time. We need to show people His love because His coming is closer than we think. Jesus came to save the lost, and we need to pray for them and seek them for His kingdom.

How do we prepare for His coming? Not through being bystanders. Not by simply going to church. Going to church is good and necessary. But we must prepare by serving. Besides prayer and study, make mission a priority. God gave us talents. Now He calls us to do small acts of daily service in a selfish world. To share the blessings that He gives us. And thus, build relationships and then invite them to follow Jesus.

True happiness comes in blessing and serving others. The more we bless and serve, the stronger we grow, and the more we become like Jesus.

In the morning, this is my prayer: *Lord, I make myself available to You today. If You need somebody to be helped, just show me. If somebody needs to hear about You, give me the opportunity, and I will do it. Show me Your plans for today. Make me a blessing. Use me.*

More importantly, keep your eyes on Jesus, the Captain of your salvation. Don't look to self, and don't monitor your spiritual growth. You will get either discouraged or proud. "Look full in His wonderful face."[3] Seek His presence and help daily, surrender your life daily, and focus on Him (not on self).

You may think that you are not making any progress. In fact, you may think that the more you pray and study and serve, the closer you try to get to Him, the worse you get. That is good news because "*Those who live nearest to Jesus* discern most clearly the frailty and sinfulness of humanity, and their only hope is in the merit of a crucified and risen Savior."[4] The closer you get to Jesus, the more you will understand your own state, so the more you will desire Him and seek Him.

Fix your eyes on Him, His cross, His promises. Choose to exercise faith. "Do not wait to *feel* that you are made whole, but say, 'I believe it; it *is* so, not because I feel it but because God has promised.' . . . Through this simple act of *believing God*, the Holy Spirit has begotten a new life in your heart. You are as a child born into the family of God, and *He loves you as He loves His Son.*"

There is no power in self. But there is infinite power in Jesus. Seek His presence, keep your eyes on Him, and choose to believe His promises. He is able. When you see Him face to face, even there, you will not understand how you could have been saved, and then you will lay your crown at His feet and acknowledge that it is He who did it all.

In the Spirit and Power

Jesus is coming very soon. There is no time to lose! He is calling each of us to a new walk with Him in His Spirit and power. And we must start that today.

When I was a child, each time I walked to school, I would pass by an older man who sold ice cream. He constantly screamed aloud, "Today you pay; tomorrow is free!" I believed him. One day I paid for chocolate and pistachio ice cream. The next day I stopped by and asked for my free ice cream.

He replied, "Today you pay; tomorrow is free."

"Well, I came yesterday, and I paid, so it should be free today."

"No, son, today you pay! For free ice cream, you need to come tomorrow."

Well, I paid again. However, I was determined to get my free ice cream the next day.

"Here I am. I want my free ice cream."

"You came again today; you need to come tomorrow."

"No, yesterday was today, and today is tomorrow."

"No, son, today is today, and today you pay."

"Then when is tomorrow?"

"Son, tomorrow never comes."

God calls us to be ready today. To pray today. Study today. Surrender today. Serve today. Seek His presence today. Today we must be filled with the Spirit.

As we look around, we know Jesus is coming; there is no more time to lose. We must be filled with God's Spirit now, today, and every day.

Only the Holy Spirit ignites the Word in our hearts. Only the Holy Spirit empowers us to practice and obey the truth. Only the Holy Spirit develops fruit within us. Only the Holy Spirit enables us for service, restores in us the image of God, and prepares us for heaven. Only the Spirit can do all these things in us.

"Abiding in Christ means a constant receiving of His Spirit, a life of unreserved surrender to His service."[5]

Don't wait for tomorrow because Jesus is at the door!

We must be people of prayer. Our churches must be houses of prayer. We must pray until . . . ! Pray to be filled with the Holy Spirit and the power to be witnesses for Him. We must go to everyone and tell them the good news. We must serve with total commitment until the day we see Him face to face.

Even so, come Lord Jesus!

[1] Ellen G. White, General Conference Bulletin, April 7, 1903, 107.

[2] Ellen G. White, *Testimonies for the Church*, vol. 7, 30.

[3] "Turn Your Eyes Upon Jesus," lyrics and music by Helen Howarth Lemmel, 1922.

[4] Ellen G. White, *The Great Controversy*, 471. Emphasis supplied.

[5] Ellen G. White, *The Desire of Ages*, 676.

SUMMARY

Pray continually. Spend time with God. Listen to Him through His Word.

Pray specifically for people. Reach them for Christ.

Joyfully say, "Here I am, Lord, send me! I will go, I will use every opportunity You give me to love and bring others to You." Do that today, and every day. Don't wait for a crisis before you seek God's presence. But more than anything, keep your eyes on Jesus, seek to be filled with His Spirit.

Put your trust in Him, His grace, His power, and His promises.

Jesus is coming soon!

Father, make us a people of prayer.
Send true power through Your Holy Spirit.
Make us witnesses for You to all the world.
And help us experience You like never before.
Amen.